AN ILLUSTRATED LITERARY GUIDE TO SHROPSHIRE

by
Gordon Dickins

Published by
Shropshire Libraries
1987

ACKNOWLEDGEMENTS

My warmest thanks go, first and foremost, to my wife Julie who drew the map, who has put up with this literary obsession of mine for so many years and who has walked a good few Shropshire miles with me in search of locations. I am indebted to many colleagues within Shropshire Libraries but especially to the staff of the Local Studies Library at Castle Gates. Also to Brenda Moore of Wellington Library, to Derek Williams of Oswestry Library, to Carol Woollard of Stirchley Library and to Miss O. S. Newman (former County Librarian) who passed on to me many additional authors' names and book titles after my first **Literary Guide** was published. For further information, ideas and suggestions I should like to thank the following: Mrs. L. Ackroyd of Shrewsbury College of Art and Technology, Mrs. Y. Brown of Ruyton XI Towns, the late Mr. Henry Green of Muxton, Mrs. E. Johnson of Market Drayton, Mr. John Laffin of Knighton, Rev. G. S. Lloyd of Atcham, Mr. Chris Moore of Madeley, Mr. James Moxon of Ashford Carbonell, Mr. Alan Sinfield of the University of Sussex, Mr. A. H. Slade of Knowbury near Ludlow and Mr. Michael Webb of Cruckton. I have given many talks and slide shows on the subject of Shropshire's literary connections and invariably, on such occasions, I have left with new information, more literary leads to follow up or locations to find as a result of members of the audience chatting to me afterwards. My thanks to them one and all and apologies for not acknowledging them individually here. A word of thanks also to Les Walton (Publications Officer for Shropshire Libraries) whose task it was to proof-read my typescript, design the cover and generally transform my badly typed original into book form.

Finally my thanks to the following people who kindly allowed me to photograph their homes: Mr. and Mrs. Bourne of Roseville, Pontesbury, Dr. Park of Plas Wilmot, Oswestry, Dr. and Mrs. Pearson of Lutwyche Hall, Mr. Poynton of Spring Cottage, Bayston Hill, Mr. and Mrs. Read of Morda Lodge, Oswestry, Mr. and Mrs. Tonks of Frogmore, Upton Magna and Mr. and Mrs. Tranter of Baxters House, Rowton.

All photographs were taken by the author unless otherwise stated.

PUBLISHER'S NOTE

The publishers would like to point out to readers that many of the houses and buildings featured in this book are privately owned. Their appearance here does not mean that they are open to the public. Appendix 2 (p.124) lists those that are open at the time of writing but readers are advised to check opening hours, etc., with the local tourist information office before visiting.

ISBN 0-903802-37-6   ©Gordon Dickins 1987   Cover: Les Walton
Published by Shropshire Libararies, London Road, Shrewsbury.
Printed in Great Britain.

CONTENTS

INTRODUCTION

When the **Literary Guide to Shropshire** was first published in 1980 I, perhaps naïvely, assumed that that was an end of it. Little did I realise that it was just the beginning of what has become a fascinating obsession which shows no sign of diminishing. So, six years later, the result is a new edition, this time photographically illustrated, containing many new entries, a few corrections and giving greater detail of both authors and the locations they have been connected with.

My interest in literary connections is longstanding and dates from cycling tours around Hardy's Wessex as a student when I realised that to actually see and experience the settings of Hardy's novels and poems added a whole new dimension to my reading and understanding of them. So it was almost inevitable, I suppose, that I should try to do the same with our own writer of the countryside, Mary Webb. This led on to other writers connected with Shropshire and the whole thing has since snowballed into a seemingly endless but highly satisfying project.

After completing the original **Literary Guide to Shropshire** I began to photograph as many of the locations as possible, initially for my own interest and enjoyment and later to supplement various talks, lectures and courses which I was involved in. To say that Shropshire is a beautiful and varied county is obviously a cliché but my forays with a camera have proved to me that it is true, not that I ever really doubted the fact. Whether or not my photographs succeed in catching the spirit of a literary location is a matter of opinion. If they fail then the fault lies with the photographer and not the Shropshire landscape! Researching and photographing the county's literary connections has given me the excuse to tramp the countryside and gain immeasurable pleasure from it. I hope that others with similar interests may gain as much as I have.

This new guide differs from the first in that, following the pattern of several national literary gazetteers, I have limited the entries to authors who are no longer living. Part 1 is an alphabetical list of authors connected with Shropshire followed, in Part 2, by a list of places. I have tried to give sufficient detail to enable anyone interested in an author's association to locate and put into context the places they lived in, visited or wrote about. Obviously in some cases there is only very sketchy information available and the guide, in any case, is not intended as an in-depth study. In an Appendix I have given a supplementary list of authors. These are, for the most part, more tenuous literary connections such as Oscar Wilde's references to Shropshire in **The Importance of Being Earnest** or works of autobiography or reminiscence which are not strictly literary. These do only comprise a selection of such works and the list is far from exhaustive. The map at the end of the book is intended to supplement the place index and to give an approximate guide to locations. Appropriate Ordnance Survey maps are essential for anyone wishing to find places of interest off the major roads.

As well as providing a gazetteer from a literary viewpoint and leading the literary pilgrim to some of the most delightful parts of the county, I hope that this book may prompt at least some readers to return to or discover for the first time the novels, poems, plays and short stories of authors who have lingered awhile in Shropshire. Many of the books mentioned are available in bookshops and libraries but others are long out of print and more difficult to obtain. The Local Studies Library at Castle Gates, Shrewsbury and the West Midlands Creative Literature Collection at Madeley Library have excellent collections which include reference copies of many of the more obscure titles.

I have included in this book as many of Shropshire's literary connections as I have been able to glean but I am confident that there are others which are still to be discovered. Many people have written to me or told me personally of authors whom I have missed, pointed out occasional errors and given me a great deal of additional information. My thanks to all of them and I hope that they, and others, will continue to share their knowledge with me.

May, 1986

The Shropshire hill country from Corndon.

Archibald Alison's church at Kenley.

PART 1: AUTHORS

ALISON, Archibald (1757-1839)

Essayist and author; rector of Kenley, near Much Wenlock. In the late 18th century he was well known for his **Essay on the Nature and Principles of Taste** (1790) and a memorial plaque in the church commemorates the fact. Alison was also a student of natural history, along the lines of Gilbert White of Selborne, and kept a nature diary. His son, also Archibald Alison (1792-1867), was born at Kenley and himself became a distinguished historian.

ALLESTREE, Richard (1619-1681)

Theological writer; born at Uppington, the son of a steward of the Newport family at Eyton on Severn, and educated at Donnington, near Wroxeter where he was a contemporary of Richard Baxter (qv). Allestree's was an old but impoverished Shropshire family, but he achieved fame with his tracts and sermons and with his major work **The Whole Duty of Man** (published at intervals between 1658 and 1670). He became Provost of Eton and Regius Professor of Divinity at Oxford and his biography was written by that same Dr. Fell, Dean of Christ Church, who was irreverently satirised by Thomas Brown (qv).

ALMEDINGEN, E. M. (1898-1971)

Novelist, biographer and children's author; born in St. Petersburg (Leningrad) and educated privately. She later attended Petrograd University and became a lecturer in English and mediaeval history there in the early 1920's. She fled to England in 1923 and settled in Shropshire, initially at Worfield, near Bridgnorth and later at Church Stretton. E. M. Almedingen was a prolific author for adults and children but she is perhaps best known for her children's novels and stories, many of which were set in her native Russia. In fact some are based on episodes in and memories of her own family's history, for example **Anna** (1972) which tells of her great grandmother. In 1941 she won the **Atlantic Review** Prize for her autobiography **Tomorrow Will Come.** Five years later she moved again, this time to Frogmore, a house on the Attingham estate between Berwick Wharf and Upton Magna, where she remained for the rest of her life. Her adult novels include **Young Catherine (1937), The Lion of the North** (1938), **Frossia** (1943), **Fair Haven** (1956), **The Little Stairway** (1960) and **Too Early Lilac** (1970). Several volumes of her poems were published, the latest being **The Unnamed Stream and Other Poems** (1965) and she wrote a number of history books and biographies. Her popular novels for children include **Little Katia** (1966), **Young Mark** (1967), **A Candle at Dusk** (1967) and many others. She was made a Fellow of the Royal Society of Literature in 1951 and received the **Book World** Festival award in 1968.

1

Frogmore, near Upton Magna; home of E. M. Almedingen.

ANSTICE, Joseph (1808-1836)

Classical scholar, essayist and hymn writer; born at Madeley Wood Hall the second son of William Anstice, a prominent local mine owner and businessman. Joseph's early childhood was spent in Madeley but he was educated at Enmore, near Bridgewater in Somerset, Westminster School and Christ Church, Oxford. At the age of just twenty-three he was invited to become Professor of Classical Literature at King's College, London. By 1835 his health was deteriorating so he retired to Torquay and spent the last few months of a tragically short life writing hymns. He wrote over fifty hymns although few are used today. Other literary works included translations into English verse from the classical poets and essays on Roman history and literature.

AUDELAY, John (early 15th century)

Poet and divine; a canon of Haughmond Abbey, near Shrewsbury. His devotional poems, written in the peace and tranquillity of this beautiful abbey, are considered interesting examples of the early Shropshire dialect. Audelay was said to have been blind and deaf, a devout man of an unworldly nature.

BARHAM, Richard Harris (1788-1845)

Author of the **Ingoldsby Legends** (1840); educated at St. Paul's School and Brasenose College, Oxford and later became a minor canon of St. Paul's. The **Ingoldsby Legends,** written in the latter part of his life, are an irreverent and often comic recreation of mediaeval legends which enjoyed a great popularity after their first publication in **Bentley's Miscellany** and in **The New Monthly Magazine.** The story of Bloudie Jack in the **Legends** serves to immortalise the famous Shrewsbury Cakes:

Oh, Pailin, Prince of Cake Compounders,
The mouth liquefies at the very sound of thy name.

Pailin's used to be the Shrewsbury School tuck shop which was renowned for these delicacies. The shop still survives in Castle Street as Halfords and a small plaque outside carries the above quotation.

BARNFIELD, Richard (1574-1627)

Poet; born at his maternal grandparents' home at Norbury, Staffordshire but brought up at The Manor House, Edgmond, near Newport. His mother died when he was only six, so his aunt, Elizabeth Skrymsher, supervised his upbringing. Having spent most of his early life at Edgmond, Barnfield went to Brasenose College, Oxford where he became a friend of the poets Thomas Watson and Michael Drayton (qv). Barnfield's first published work was **The Affectionate Shepherd** (1594), a pastoral poem based on the second eclogue of Virgil. This was followed by **Cynthia, With Certain Sonnets** (1595) and further poems in 1598. Two of his poems appeared in **The Passionate Pilgrim** (1599) which was an anthology published by William Jaggard and with a title page attributing the work to Shakespeare. **The Encomion of Lady Pecunia** (1599) was Barnfield's last published piece, a poem satirising the power of money. Later he enjoyed the life of a country gentleman at Barlaston in Staffordshire.

BATHER, Lucy (1836-1864)

Children's author, known as 'Aunt Lucy'; born at Fulham, the daughter of Dr. Blomfield, Bishop of London. She married Arthur Henry Bather of The Hall, Meole Brace, Shrewsbury where she spent the rest of her short life. Lucy Bather wrote stories for children together with a more substantial work called **Footprints on the Sands of Time: Biographies for Young People** (1860).

BAXTER, Richard (1615-1691)

Religious writer; born at Rowton, near High Ercall at the home of his mother's parents and baptised at High Ercall. In fact he spent the first ten years of his life here and during this time received a somewhat meagre education at the hands of four masters in the space of six years. Baxter later said that they were all ignorant, two of them being immoral and the last a drunkard – hardly an auspicious start for a man who was later to be offered a bishopric (he refused it) and who was to write **The Saint's Everlasting Rest** (1650). In February 1626 he was removed to his parents' home (now called Baxter's House) in Eaton Constantine but here his schooling was no better than at Rowton, the masters being a sorry succession of bullies, drunks and incompetents. In fact Richard Baxter seems to have been singularly unlucky in his education with the exception of his next school, which was at Donnington in the neighbouring parish of Wroxeter. This school was under the patronage of the Newport family of Eyton on Severn and a fellow pupil was Richard Allestree (qv) from Uppington. Baxter had hoped to follow Allestree's example and go to university but his schoolmaster persuaded his parents to send their son to Ludlow Castle, where he

Ludlow Castle, where Richard Baxter received an unusual education.

In this house
lived
The learned & eloquent
RICHARD BAXTER
1640 - 1641

Baxter's House, Bridgnorth.

would study under Richard Wicksted who was Chaplain to the Council of the Welsh Marches. Baxter, now aged sixteen, soon regretted this for he found Wickstead to be a poor teacher with only a superficial knowledge. He certainly seems to have been highly critical of life in Ludlow, recalling later that the town was "full of temptations" and "much given to tipling and excess". However, one aspect of his education was successful – he was taught to play cards by the Clerk of the Kitchen (reputedly the best player at the castle) so well that he was eventually able to beat his tutor. Baxter promptly gave up the game, realising that he was too good for his own best interests. He returned home where Sir Richard Newport set him to teach at his old Donnington school for three months before moving to London. By this time, as well as being struck by the religious integrity and influence of his father, he had come into contact and had been impressed by a group of Nonconformist ministers in Shrewsbury.

In December 1638 Baxter was ordained deacon at Worcester and granted a licence to teach at Dudley, where he stayed for just nine months. He moved to Bridgnorth in 1640 as assistant minister to William Madstart at St. Leonard's Church, living in a tiny house, which can still be seen, opposite. He later dedicated the second part of **The Saint's Everlasting Rest** to the people of Bridgnorth even though he found them "a very ignorant, deadhearted people". He stayed less than a year having received little encouragement. Five years later, in 1646, Parliamentary forces, with whom he sympathised, came to Bridgnorth and burned the church, the castle and the town. Baxter had moved to Kidderminster and after the Civil War, during which time he was an itinerant chaplain in the Parliamentarian army, he returned as minister and as a writer of increasing stature. During the Restoration he was ill-treated under Charles II and James II and was imprisoned by the infamous Judge Jeffreys on the charge of libelling the Church in his **Paraphrase of the New Testament** (1685). Baxter is now considered to have been one of the founding fathers of Nonconformity and is remembered for his devotional books. His autobiography **Reliquiae Baxterianae** was published posthumously in 1696. Richard Baxter always retained a fond allegiance to Shropshire and to Shrewsbury especially where a close friend William Rowley, the draper and alderman, had a fine house built (Rowley's House, now the Museum).

BENSON, Stella (1892-1933)

Novelist; born at Lutwyche Hall on Wenlock Edge. Her mother was a younger sister of the novelist Mary Cholmondeley (qv) from Hodnet. Stella, a delicate child, was educated privately at home and then on the Continent. Prior to the First World War she worked in the East End of London for The Charity Organisation Society and took a deep interest in women's suffrage. She opened a shop in Hoxton and remained there until 1917 during which time she wrote her first two novels, **I Pose** (1915) and **This is the End** (1917). In June 1918 she left for the U.S.A. and on arrival took menial jobs before obtaining a post as tutor at the University of California and later as editorial reader for the University Press. In 1920 she decided to return to England and undertook an eighteen month, adventurous journey via the Far East, during which she worked in a mission school and a hospital. In China she met John O'Gorman Anderson, a Customs worker, and they were married in London in 1921. Their honeymoon, which they spent crossing America in a Ford car, was described in Stella's book

Lutwyche Hall, birthplace of novelist Stella Benson.

The Little World (1925). They returned to China and lived in obscure and sometimes politically dangerous areas. Stella continued to write novels and stories most of which are now long since forgotten – **Goodbye, Stranger** (1926), **The Man Who Missed the Bus** (1928) and **Tobit Transplanted** (1930) which won the Femina Vie Heureuse Prize. Martin Seymour-Smith in his **Novels and Novelists: a Guide to the World of Fiction** (1980) states that she was "possessed of a fine imagination whose qualities have as yet gone largely unrecognised." Two volumes of Stella Benson's short stories were published, **Hope Against Hope** (1931) and **Christmas Formula** (1932) and she was the author of numerous other stories and travel sketches. She was living in Hongay in the province of Tongking when she died of pneumonia just before her forty-first birthday in December 1933. Stella was a friend of the novelist Winifred Holtby and, through her, of Vera Brittain and there is a moving account of the news of her death and the effect it had upon these two writers in Vera Brittain's second volume of autobiography **Testament of Experience** (1957). Stella's brother George Reginald Benson who inherited Lutwyche Hall, was the author of one novel, **Brother Wolf** (1933).

BETJEMAN, John (1906-1984)

Poet, essayist and architectural critic. Betjeman wrote **The Shell Guide to Shropshire** (1951) having presumably spent some time in the county. Betjeman is best linked with Shropshire on the strength of one poem, much anthologised, called **A Shropshire Lad** about Captain Webb the famous Channel swimmer from Dawley.

BETTY, William Henry West (1791-1874)

Child actor of great fame and fashion; born in Shrewsbury. Betty played major Shakespearean roles from the age of twelve and was popularly known as 'Young Roscius'. However, his acting career was short and he retired from the stage in 1824. His father had died at the family home, Pym's Farm, Wem in 1811 and Betty himself returned to this part of Shropshire, died in 1874 and was buried at Loppington.

BOTFIELD, Beriah (1807-1863)

Bibliographer; born at Earl's Ditton near Cleobury Mortimer. His mother, Charlotte, was the daughter of the botanist William Withering and the Botfield family was descended from the Botevilles and the Thynnes. He was educated at Harrow and Christ Church, Oxford and was, initially, a scientist and botanist. Later in life bibliography became his major interest, his most important work being a bibliography of early manuscript literature called **Praefationes et Epistolae Editionibus Principibus Auctorum Veterum Praepositae** (1861). He was the author of other works of bibliography together with pieces on archaeology and botany and was an occasional contributor to **The Gentleman's Magazine.** Beriah Botfield was returned as M.P. for Ludlow in the General Elections of 1840, 1841 and 1857 and had a Shropshire home at Decker Hall near Shifnal.

BRAY, Thomas (1658-1730)

Religious writer and co-founder of the Society for Promoting Christian Knowledge

(S.P.C.K.); born at Marton in a half timbered house known as Bray's Tenement and baptised at Chirbury. Bray was educated at Oswestry Grammar School, Hart Hall, Oxford and All Souls' College, Oxford. He was a curate in Bridgnorth for a short time but began his writing career when rector of Sheldon in Warwickshire, producing theological works primarily. Thomas Bray is included here not only for his own writings but also for his work with the S.P.C.K. and his scheme to set up libraries for parochial clergymen who were too poor to buy their own books. At the time of his death he had established eighty such libraries in England and Wales and thirty-nine in America where he worked for a time. The last years of his life were spent in the East End of London as vicar of St. Botolph, Aldgate. In 1901 a memorial tablet was placed in St. Michael's Church, Chirbury commemorating his early life in the parish.

BRONTË, Patrick (1777-1861)

Minor poet and father of Charlotte, Emily, Anne and Branwell Brontë. He was born in Ireland, the son of a farm labourer, came to England to pursue his studies and went to St. John's College, Cambridge – he was ordained in 1806. A Cambridge friend was John Nunn who became a curate at St. Chad's in Shrewsbury. He told Brontë that there was a vacancy for a curate in Wellington, Bronte applied and was duly appointed in January 1809 to All Saints' Church. Wellington at that time was a growing town in the mining district and Brontë, who became a well known figure, witnessed and did what he could to alleviate the squalor and poverty of the workers. Although the area was scarred by mining and industry, the Wrekin nearby remained unspoiled and Brontë delighted in walking on this famous Shropshire hill. A fellow curate was William Morgan who had connections with many leading Methodists including Mary Fletcher, widow of John Fletcher (qv) and who was well known for doing all she could to advance young and worthy curates to continue the work of John Wesley. Brontë was introduced to her by William Morgan and she proved instrumental in finding him a post in Yorkshire, as curate at Dewsbury. His Wellington curacy ended in December 1809. While he was in Wellington, Patrick Brontë wrote two small volumes of poetry, **Cottage Poems** and **The Rural Minstrel,** both of which were published by Houlstons of Market Square, Wellington. Houlstons (now Hobsons, in the same premises) were among the most prolific publishers of religious tracts, poems and broadsheets in the early nineteenth century, a time of great evangelical fervour, as well as many of the children's moral tales by Mrs. Sherwood (qv).

BROOKS, Charles William Shirley (1816-1874)

Author, essayist and editor of **Punch;** born in London but articled to his uncle, Charles Sabine, an Oswestry solicitor. Brooks remained in Oswestry for five years, passed his law exams, but never became a solicitor. By the early 1850's he was working in London for **The Morning Chronicle** and was sent to Russia, Syria and Egypt to report on the state of labour and the poor. He also wrote articles for **Ainsworth's Magazine** and began to sign himself Shirley Brooks. Brooks had many literary friends in London and he achieved considerable success with several of his plays being performed on the West End stage – **The Creole, or Love's Fetters** (1847), **Anything For a Change** (1848), **Daughter of the Stars** (1850), **The Exposition: a Scandinavian Sketch** (1851) and others. He was a leader writer on

All Saints' Church, Wellington. Patrick Brontë was curate here.

The Illustrated London News and was associated with many other leading periodicals. He also tried his hand at novel writing with **Aspen Court: a Story of Our Own Time** (1855) and **The Gordian Knot** (1858), this latter being illustrated by Tenniel and with passages recalling the author's Oswestry days. Shirley Brooks wrote for **Punch** from 1851 onwards and became its editor in 1870. He died in London in February 1874.

BROWN, Thomas (1663-1704)

Poet, satirist and translator; said to have been born in Shifnal although it is possible that Newport was his place of birth, since a Thomas Brown, son of William and Dorothy Brown, was baptised at Newport in 1663. Thomas was the son of a farmer/tanner who died when the boy was only eight. He attended Newport Free Grammar School and then went on to Christ Church, Oxford. Here he was threatened with expulsion by the famous Dr. Fell unless he could translate a particular Latin epigram. Brown obliged, as follows, and in doing so added to his own fame as well as immortalising the good doctor:

I do not love thee, Dr. Fell,
The reason why I cannot tell;
But this I know, and know full well,
I do not love thee, Dr. Fell.

Brown survived Oxford, and Dr. Fell, and settled in London where he worked as a translator and hack writer. His **Amusements Serious and Comical** (1700) provided entertaining sketches of London life. Much of his own work took the form of satirical poems and pamphlets which, together with his licentious lifestyle, often got him into trouble with authority. Nevertheless, after death he achieved what many aspire to and was buried in Westminster Abbey.

BROWNE, Isaac Hawkins (1705-1760)

Poet; born at Burton on Trent and educated at Westminster School and Trinity College, Cambridge. Browne settled in Shropshire at Badger (his home, Badger Hall, was demolished in the 1950's;) and was returned as M.P. for Much Wenlock in 1744 and 1747. However, although known in literary circles as a great wit and conversationalist it seems that he did not carry these qualities into the House of Commons for Dr. Johnson said of him, "Browne, one of the first wits of this country, got into Parliament and never opened his mouth". Browne gained literary popularity with **Design and Beauty** (1734) and **A Pipe of Tobacco** (1736), the latter being an ode in imitation of Pope and Swift. His principal work was **De Animi Immortalitate** (1754) which was much praised by contemporary scholars. Browne's poems were collected and published in two volumes in 1768 by his son Isaac Hawkins Browne the younger (qv).

BROWNE, Isaac Hawkins (1745-1818)

Essayist; born at Badger Hall and educated at Westminster School and Hertford College, Oxford. After travelling abroad he settled on the Badger estate and was made Sheriff of the county in 1783. In 1784 he was returned as M.P. for Bridgnorth and represented the town in this capacity for twenty-eight years. His **Essays, Religious and Moral** (1815) were published anonymously at first, although his name was added to later editions. **Essays on Subjects of Important Inquiry in Metaphysics, Morals and Religion** (1822) were published posthumously.

BURNE, Charlotte Sophia (1850-1923)

Folklorist; born at Moreton Vicarage in Staffordshire, close to the Shropshire border. Although Staffordshire born, her main interest was in the folklore and customs of Shropshire and she became an assistant to Georgina F. Jackson (qv) who was working on her unique **Shropshire Word Book** (1879-81). Charlotte Burne, who came to live at Edgmond, continued Miss Jackson's work after her death and produced her own **Shropshire Folk Lore** (1883). This impressive and comprehensive work, one of the first of its kind in this country, fascinated and intrigued Mary Webb (qv) who drew upon it in her own novels of the Shropshire countryside.

BURNEY, Charles (1726-1814)

Author and composer; born in Raven Street, Shrewsbury and baptised at St. Mary's Church. His parents moved to Chester when he was a child, so he was looked after by a nurse in Condover before being sent to school in Chester himself where he showed great musical talent. He returned to Shrewsbury in 1741 and three years later moved to London to study under Dr. Arne, a leading musician. Charles Burney became a friend of many literary and artistic people such as Dr. Johnson, Garrick and Reynolds and travelled extensively abroad. He had a long career as a musician, composer and author of books on musical subjects, such as his **History of Music** which was published in four volumes between 1776 and 1789. He also wrote accounts of his travels abroad in Germany, France, Italy and the Low Countries. His daughter Frances was the novelist Fanny Burney, author of **Evelina** (1778).

BUTLER, Samuel (1612-1680)

Poet and satirist; born at Strensham in Worcestershire and educated at the King's School, Worcester. Very little is known about his life apart from a few sketchy details. Charles II is known to have had a high opinion of Butler's great religious satire **Hudibras** (1663-1678) and awarded him an annual pension of £100, although the writer still died in poverty. Butler began **Hudibras** while lodging in Holborn around 1658. In 1661 he is recorded as being at Ludlow Castle as steward to Richard Vaughan, Earl of Carberry. During the Civil War the castle had been captured by Parliamentarians and the contents sold, but during the Restoration, when the Court of the Marches was revived, Carberry (the President) undertook to make the castle inhabitable again. Part of Samuel Butler's work at the castle was towards this end, with account books apparently showing him making payments to craftsmen working on the repairs. He is supposed to have married around this time and was certainly still working on **Hudibras,** a satire ridiculing religious hypocrisy, while at Ludlow. He gave up his stewardship in January 1662 and the first part of **Hudibras** was published in December of the same year.

Ludlow Castle; Samuel Butler was steward here in the 1660's.

BUTLER, Samuel (1835-1902)

Novelist and satirist; born in Nottinghamshire, the son of a vicar. His father was a cruel man who beat his son daily and was duly hated for this. Samuel Butler was to recreate the pain and despair of his childhood years in his final novel **The Way of All Flesh** (1903). At the age of twelve he was sent to Shrewsbury School, then under the headship of Dr. Kennedy (Dr. Skinner in the novel). At Shrewsbury he was able to visit his aunt and uncle, the Bathers, at their Meole Brace home. Samuel did not enjoy the hard life at Shrewsbury School under the fearsome Dr. Kennedy but he did at least escape his father's merciless beatings. Again, he recalled his Shrewsbury schooldays in **The Way of All Flesh** although his portrayal of the school is generally considered to be somewhat less than objective. He left in 1854 for Cambridge after which he travelled to New Zealand where he succeeded as a sheep breeder (described in his **A First Year in Canterbury Settlement** (1863)). He returned to England and wrote one of his best known novels **Erewhon** (1872), set in a fictitious land, a pointed satire of many of the customs, institutions and attitudes of the time, with which he was incensed. This was followed by **The Fair Haven** (1873) and a series of books on controversial scientific subjects. In 1896 he completed his **Life and Letters of Dr. Samuel Butler,** his grandfather and earlier head of Shrewsbury School. He translated **The Iliad** and **The Odyssey** in 1898 and 1900 respectively and concluded that the author was a woman and wrote **Shakespeare's Sonnets Reconsidered** (1899). **Erewhon Revisited** (1901) was his last novel published in his lifetime, **The Way of All Flesh** being published posthumously.

BYFORD-JONES, Wilfred (1907-1977)

Author and journalist; although not Shropshire born he came to know and love the county and lived for some time at Lower Hall, Beckbury before retiring to Machynlleth. Wilfred Byford-Jones, who often used the pen name 'Quaestor', worked for many years on the **Express and Star** and **Shropshire Star** being associate editor of the former. He wrote many articles on Shropshire people and places, some of which were collected in his **Severn Valley Stories** (1967). Before the war, a local best seller was his first collection of essays, **Both Sides of the Severn** (1933) which was followed by **The Shropshire Haunts of Mary Webb** (1948).

CARDUS, Neville (1889-1975)

Prominent music critic and writer on cricket; born at Rusholme, Manchester. Cardus came from a working class background and was largely self-educated. He began work as a clerk in a marine insurance office and, during his seven years with the company, started to write essays and articles and to attend the free lectures at Manchester University. To escape from Manchester he applied, in January 1912, for the post of assistant cricket coach at Shrewsbury School and was appointed. His **Autobiography** (1947) gives a warm, vivid and often humorous account of his experiences at Shrewsbury including the delightful episode when the dour Wainwright, former Yorkshire and England player and School coach, admonished the headmaster (Cyril Alington), at the top of his voice and in fulsome Yorkshire dialect, for riding his bicycle across the sacred cricket square. In 1914 Alington appointed Cardus as his secretary

The original Shrewsbury School, Castle Gates.

and when he was given the headship of Eton in 1916 it was intended that his secretary should follow. However, due to the possibility of conscription (having been rejected initially due to short sightedness) Cardus was unable to take up his post returning, instead, to Manchester, where he embarked upon what was to become a most successful career in journalism.

CHOLMONDELEY, Mary (1859-1925)

Novelist; born in Hodnet, the daughter of Hugh Cholmondeley the rector. The Cholmondeleys were an old Shropshire family and several had been rectors of Hodnet. Her paternal grandmother inherited Hodnet Hall and in her autobiography **Under One Roof** (1917) she tells of how the formidable old lady, when travelling by the new-fangled train, insisted on her own carriage being lifted onto a railway wagon so that she could travel in privacy. Reginald Heber (qv) the poet and hymn writer was another ancestor of the Cholmondeleys. Mary was the eldest daughter and third child in a family of eight and from an early age had made up stories to tell to her brothers and sisters for their entertainment. She began to write seriously in her late teens and her first novel was **Her Evil Genius** which was followed by **The Danvers Jewels** (1886). A shy girl, she nevertheless mixed in literary circles in London after achieving some success with her novels. In 1896 her father had to give up his living in Hodnet through ill health so the family moved in the first instance to Condover Hall, which they had inherited from Reginald Cholmondeley (who had hosted the visits of Mark Twain (qv)). They stayed here only a few months before selling up and moving to London. In 1899 Mary's best known novel **Red Pottage** was published and caused something of a sensation at the time because of its pointed satire. In addition to novels Mary wrote essays, articles and short stories.

CHURCHYARD, Thomas (1520-1604)

Elizabethan courtier and poet; born in Shrewsbury where he lived until the age of nineteen. He became a professional soldier in 1541 and led an adventurous, and at times dangerous, life. He left the army in 1572 two years after coming very close to being executed in the Netherlands, in between his periods of soldiering abroad he spent time as a courtier. He had written pageants for Elizabeth I in 1574 and 1578 but she took offence at a passage in his book **Churchyard's Choise** (1578) and he found a sudden need to go to Scotland for three years to escape her wrath. Elizabeth did eventually allow him a small pension. As a poet he continued to write until an advanced age but in more or less the same style so that, latterly, he was considered rather old fashioned. In fact Spenser referred to him, in **Colin Clout's Come Home Again** (1595), as " . . . old Palaemon that had sung so long until quite hoarse he grew". Churchyard's main prose work was **The Worthiness of Wales** (1587) which anticipated Drayton in many respects as an antiquarian survey and which contains a long and affectionate description of Shrewsbury. He is generally considered at his best in a much earlier work, **The Legend of Shore's Wife** (1563).

CLAYTON, John (1885-1939)

Real name Henry Bertram Law Webb, husband of the novelist and poet Mary Webb (qv) and nephew of Captain Matthew Webb of Dawley (the first man to swim the

Present day Shrewsbury School playing fields.

Unitarian Church, Shrewsbury.

English Channel). Henry Webb was a classical scholar and teacher, and at the time he met Mary was working on a volume of philosophic essays called **The Silences of the Moon** (1911). These were published under his own name, but after his wife's death he used the pen-name John Clayton for translations and for his own historical novels such as **The Gold of Toulouse** (1932), **Dew in April** (1934) and **The Silver Swan** (1939). He was tragically killed while climbing Scafell in August 1939.

COKE, Desmond (1879-1959)

Minor novelist and writer of stories for boys; educated at Shrewsbury School. **The Bending of a Twig** (1906) was intended as a parody of the traditional school story and achieved a brief popularity. The story tells of the experiences of its hero, Lycidas Marsh, at Shrewsbury School and is of course based on memories of his own schooldays there.

COLERIDGE, Samuel Taylor (1772-1834)

Poet, philosopher and literary critic; came to Shrewsbury in late 1797 when he acted as locum to Rev. Dr. Rowe at the High Street Unitarian Church. Coleridge was already an established poet at this time, having met Wordsworth two years before and worked out their joint contributions to **Lyrical Ballads** (1798). Possibly Coleridge's greatest contribution to this was his **Rime of the Ancient Mariner** which he is said to have read at a literary evening in Mardol. He came to Shrewsbury in December 1797, contemplating a career in the church since he could not make a living just by his writing. The wealthy Wedgwood family offered him £100 to help him out of his financial difficulties, but he declined the offer as it would only delay matters. On Sunday, 14th January, 1798, he preached a probationary sermon. Among the congregation was the young William Hazlitt (qv), then aged about nineteen, who had walked all the way from his home in Wem in order to hear him. Coleridge in fact visited Hazlitt's home (William's father was a minister at Wem) in Noble Street, Wem but within a day or two of preaching in Shrewsbury received a letter from Josiah Wedgwood offering him an annuity of £150 per year on condition that he gave up his ministerial career. Coleridge gladly accepted this opportunity, much to the disappointment of Hazlitt who had hoped to have him as a neighbour.

COTTON, Roger (fl. 1596)

Poet; born at Alkington, Whitchurch from a literary family and was probably educated at the newly founded free school in the town. A religious, literary man, he was devoted to study of the scriptures. Cotton married a Katherine Jenks of Market Drayton. His two main devotional poems, for which he is best known, were **An Armor of Proofe** (1596) and **A Spirituall Song** (1596).

DARWIN, Charles Robert (1809-1882)

Naturalist and author famous for promotion of the theory of natural selection. Darwin was born at The Mount in Shrewsbury, the fifth child of Dr. Robert Waring Darwin and Susannah (eldest daughter of Josiah Wedgwood). They were Unitarians and worshipped at the High Street Unitarian Church where there is a commemorative tablet to

Charles, even though he was baptised at St. Chad's Church. He was educated at home initially and then at a day school kept by the Rev. Case at 13 Claremont Hill. In 1818 Charles was sent as a boarder to Shrewsbury School, then in the original building at Castle Gates, where conditions for the boys were decidedly austere. The building now houses Shrewsbury Library and has been recently restored to its Elizabethan splendour. At the front entrance is an imposing statue of Darwin erected in 1897. At the age of sixteen Charles was sent to Edinburgh to study medicine, but this was not to his liking, so after two years he went to Cambridge, his father now intending him to become a parson. The invitation to sail on the Beagle as a naturalist, in 1831, of course thwarted the ecclesiastical career, but set up Charles Darwin to become, in the following years, one of the most influential figures of the century. Darwin is not, strictly speaking, a literary figure but the impact of his discoveries and theories was so great in scientific, religious, philosophic and literary fields that he has to be included here. His two most famous works were **On the Origin of Species by Means of Natural Selection** (1859) and **The Descent of Man** (1871).

Charles Darwin's birthplace at The Mount, Shrewsbury.

Darwin's Statue outside the old Shrewsbury School.

DEFOE, Daniel (1660-1731)

Novelist and prolific pamphleteer; born in London. Defoe had a chequered career, at one time being imprisoned and pilloried for writing a satirical pamphlet on dissent. He is best known for his two major novels, **Robinson Crusoe** (1719) and **Moll Flanders** (1722). His **Tour Through the Whole Island of Great Britain** (1724-27) was a three volume guide book to the country, based on a number of journeys, and giving a lively view of life at the time. Defoe passed through Shropshire on his travels and the **Tour** gives descriptions of Whitchurch and Shrewsbury. **Memoirs of a Cavalier** (1720) is a supposedly factual account of Royalist campaigns by a Shropshire-born soldier according to Defoe. It has been suggested that the soldier was Andrew, son of Richard Newport of High Ercall, but this is speculation and the book, which again contains descriptions of Shrewsbury, is more likely another work of fiction by Defoe.

DE QUINCEY, Thomas (1785-1859)

Essayist and critic; born in Manchester and educated at Manchester Grammar School and Worcester College, Oxford, although he gained no degree. His addiction to opium had begun while he was at Oxford and he wrote his **Confessions of an English Opium Eater** (1822) for **Blackwood's Magazine.** He was the author of a wide range of essays on many different subjects, biographical articles on Wordsworth, Coleridge and Lamb as well as fictional tales and many literary pieces. In 1802 he had a brief but memorable stay in Shrewsbury, at The Lion Hotel, en route to London from Wales. Instead of being given a normal bedroom he was offered the strange disused ballroom with chandeliers wrapped in paper and space for two orchestras. The weird surroundings together with a wild and windy night, obviously played upon his imagination or subconscious and he passed a fitful night dreaming, as he later wrote, that the ballroom was thronged with people and the orchestra playing. The recollection of this nightmare in the morning preyed upon his emotions, for he was undergoing some kind of personal crisis already, and he had ominous thoughts about his trip to London. However, he survived his stay in Shrewsbury and arrived safely in the capital.

DICKENS, Charles (1812-1870)

The great Victorian novelist visited the county on several occasions and stayed three times at The Lion Hotel in Shrewsbury. His first visit was in the company of Hablot K. Brown ('Phiz'), the illustrator of some of his books, in 1838. In 1852 he returned, this time with the novelist and occasional co-writer Wilkie Collins. They presented and performed in a play called **Mr Nightingale's Diary** at the Music Hall. Six years later in August 1858 Dickens gave one of his famous readings from his novels and tales at the same venue and, while he was in the district, visited the Roman excavations at Wroxeter. The result of this was an article in **All the Year Round** in May 1859 on the Roman occupation and the Wroxeter excavations and discoveries. As well as these visits to Shrewsbury Dickens stayed in Tong and Newport and both places made important contributions to two of his best known novels. In **The Old Curiosity Shop** (1841) Little Nell and her grandfather, desperately trying to escape the clutches of the

The Lion Hotel, Shrewsbury.

evil Quilp, leave London and travel north, passing through the industrial nightmare which was the Black Country. Eventually they find refuge in a small, picturesque village with a distant view of " . . . the blue Welsh mountains far away". That village was almost certainly Tong. Dickens had stayed here at an old coaching inn on the London to Chester mail coach run, and seen the church and village nearby. The church certainly made a great impression on him for he described it in full and accurate detail in the novel:

> It was a very aged, ghostly place; the church had been built many hundreds of years ago, and had once had a convent or monastery attached; for arches in ruins, remains of oriel windows, and fragments of blackened walls, were yet standing . . . Some part of the edifice had been a baronial chapel, and here were effigies of warriors stretched upon their beds of stone with folded hands, cross-legged – those who had fought in the Holy Wars – girded with their swords, and cased in armour as they had lived.

The novelist's son Sir Henry Dickens came to see Tong for himself in 1877, seven years after his father's death. A few miles north of Tong is Newport and it was while he was staying there at The Bear Hotel (now Beaumaris House, part of Adams Grammar School) that Charles Dickens heard a rather sad local story. Elizabeth Parker of Chetwynd House in Newport had been jilted on the very day of her wedding. Totally

Tong Church; where Dickens' Little Nell found refuge.

24

distraught she became a virtual recluse, living in the upper rooms of her house while the lower floor was kept unfurnished apart from one room in which her wedding cake was kept as a poignant relic. The story goes that she made just one public appearance after this, at a county ball in Newport where she hoped to meet the man who should have been her husband – but she was disappointed again. Elizabeth Parker's sad history obviously gave Dickens the idea for the fantastic Miss Havisham in his later novel **Great Expectations** (1861). The house he describes in the novel is not Chetwynd House but Restoration House in Rochester, Kent but there is no disputing that Miss Havisham is based on the unfortunate Shropshire lady. There are two final, albeit minor, Shropshire connections or references in the novels of Charles Dickens. The character Sydney Carton in **A Tale of Two Cities** (1859) was supposed to be an old boy of Shrewsbury School while in **Bleak House** (1853) 'the man from Shropshire' is a pathetic, shadowy figure who forlornly haunts the Court of Chancery in the vain hope of receiving justice.

DISRAELI, Benjamin (1804-1881)

Statesman and novelist; M.P. for Shrewsbury from 1841 to 1847. Disraeli was a novelist of considerable stature, dealing with contemporary social and political issues in his works. Three of his best known novels – **Coningsby** (1844), **Sybil** (1845) and **Tancred** (1847) – were written while he was representing Shrewsbury in Parliament. He does not appear to have spent very much time in Shrewsbury during this period, a fact which suggests that his seat was mainly one of convenience. Disraeli had been elected M.P. for Maidstone at the 1837 election but had to find an alternative seat for the next election of 1841. His friend Lord Forester helped him to gain the nomination for Shrewsbury which was thought to be a safe seat. However, he did experience difficulties in the run in to the election, due to one of his opponents advertising that he was £22,000 in debt. Disraeli denied this of course and was duly elected, although later it was discovered that his financial affairs were in disarray. While canvassing in Shrewsbury in June 1841 Disraeli stayed, as have so many other illustrious visitors to the town, at The Lion Hotel. He gave up his Shrewsbury seat when, for social prestige and political advancement, he took a house in Buckinghamshire and stood for that county in the General Election of 1847.

DOVASTON, John F. M. (1782-1854)

Minor poet and naturalist; born at The Nursery, West Felton and educated at Oswestry School, Shrewsbury School and Oxford. He was a friend of Bewick, the famous engraver. Following the death of his father in 1808 he spent the rest of his life at The Nursery in literary retirement, writing light verse and occasional articles on natural history. **Fitz-Gwarine** (1812) was his version of the Fitzwarine legend, a tale of love, treachery and tragedy at nearby Whittington Castle.

DOYLE, Arthur Conan (1859-1930)

Novelist and creator of the great fictional detective Sherlock Holmes; born in Edinburgh and studied medicine at Edinburgh University. He later practised at Southsea from 1882 to 1890. Due to family financial restraints Doyle had to try and find work as a medical assistant during his course of study. In 1878, after two unsuccessful attempts in Sheffield and London, he was taken on by a Dr. Elliot of Ruyton-of-the-Eleven-Towns, a large village between Baschurch and Oswestry. He spent four months here and for the most part it was quiet and uneventual, allowing him plenty of time for personal reading and study. However, one day when the doctor was out he was called to an emergency at one of the large houses in the village where some of the gentry had been fooling around with an old cannon. It had been fired but burst apart and a bystander ended up with a large chunk of metal in his head. Doyle had no alternative but to remove it, managed to staunch the bleeding and dress the wound and generally did his own reputation a great deal of good. In his **Memories and Recollections** (1924) he said that his stay in Ruyton was a happy one and that he had pleasant memories of Dr. Elliot and his wife. John Dickson Carr, on the other hand, in his biography of the writer, published in 1949, said that the student was often angered by the doctor's quick temper and that, for his four months' work, was not paid a penny. While it can hardly be said that Shropshire had any formative influence on Arthur Conan Doyle as a writer it is nevertheless an interesting literary connection for all that.

DRAYTON, Michael (1563-1631)

Poet; born at Hartshill near Atherstone in Warwickshire. He wrote eclogues and sonnets in the style of Spenser, but is most famous for his long topographical poem **Polyolbion** (1622). This sets out to show the beauties and glories of the countryside together with passages of local history, folklore and natural history and includes descriptions of Shropshire.

DUPPA, Richard (1770-1831)

Author and artist; lived at Culmington near Ludlow and wrote numerous books on art and artists as well as pamphlets on miscellaneous subjects. In 1816 he illustrated, edited and printed **Dr. Johnson's Diary of a Journey into North Wales in 1774.**

EAGER, Frances (d. 1978)

Popular children's author; lived at Ingram's Hall, The Schools, Shrewsbury.

EVANS, Simon (1895-1940)

Novelist and short story writer. After the First World War he came to Shropshire and settled in Cleobury Mortimer, country living having been recommended to him as an aid to recuperation from the effects of wartime poison gas. He became a country postman and walked eighteen miles or so each day — in the process he quickly grew to know and love the people and scenery of this part of the county and they provided him with material for the articles and stories which he was beginning to write during the 1920's. By 1930 some of these had been published and he had taken part in radio programmes. Then followed collections of stories such as **Round About the Crooked Steeple** (1931), **At Abdon Burf** (1932) and **More Tales From Round About the Crooked Steeple** (1935) all set in or around Cleobury Mortimer (whose church of course has a crooked steeple) and the Clee Hills. His one novel,

Cleobury Mortimer's crooked steeple.

27

The bleak summit of Brown Clee.

Applegarth (1936) is said to be partly autobiographical and, like all his work, uses a mixture of real and fictional places. Simon Evans finally succumbed to the effects of the poison gas and died in Selly Oak Hospital, Birmingham on 8th August 1940.

EYTON, Robert William (1815-1881)

Historian and antiquarian; son of Rev. John Eyton of Wellington and Eyton. Lived at Tong during his childhood and was educated at Bridgnorth Grammar School. He was ordained in 1839 and became Rector of Ryton, near Shifnal, where he remained for twenty-two years. He researched and wrote his major work **The Antiquities of Shropshire** (1860) during this time. Ill health prevented him from bringing the work up to date. He eventually left Shropshire and resumed his writing, although no longer on Shropshire history.

FARQUHAR, George (1678-1707)

Soldier and dramatist of the school of Congreve; born in Londonderry. Farquhar was in the army before he became an actor and dramatist and was sent to Shrewsbury to help raise men to fight in the War of the Spanish Succession. He is said to have stayed at The Raven Hotel in the town (now demolished). **The Recruiting Officer** (1706), one of his best comedies, is almost certainly based on his own experiences in Shrewsbury and is dedicated to "all friends round the Wrekin". George Farquhar seems to have been a pleasant, high spirited character and certainly good humour is an ingredient of this play. His last play, **The Beaux' Stratagem** (1707) is usually

The Raven Hotel, Shrewsbury (photo: Shropshire Libraries).

ranked with it but he died in poverty shortly after its first successful staging.

FIENNES, Celia (1662-1741)

Intrepid Englishwoman who travelled the country on horseback and wrote eye-witness accounts of the life and customs of the time; born at Newton Toney near Salisbury. Her journal was not published until 1888 under the title **Through England on a Side Saddle in the Time of William and Mary.** The complete, definitive edition was published in 1947 as **The Journeys of Celia Fiennes.** During her travels she visited every county in England including Shropshire and her record of her adventures, experiences and observations provides us now with a most entertaining account of life in town and country in the late seventeenth century. 1698 was the year of her "great journey to Newcastle and to Cornwall" and she reached Shropshire on her way south from Manchester. Her arrival in the county was nearly memorable for the wrong reasons because a few miles from Whitchurch she and her two women companions were followed and jostled by a couple of unsavoury looking characters whom she was convinced were highwaymen. Fortunately there were people working in the fields and a steady stream of travellers was coming away from Whitchurch market, so the highwaymen were thwarted in their apparent intentions and gave up their pursuit. She arrived in Whitchurch and saw two fine gardens, one belonging to an apothecary the other at The Crown Inn, before continuing on her way to Shrewsbury. Here she describes many of the main features of the county town

Whittington Castle built by the Fitzwarine family.   *Old Vicarage, Madeley; once the home of John Fletcher.*

including the castle, the river and the bridges one of which, she says, " . . . had some few houses built on it, as London Bridge". She notes too the Free Schools in Castle Gates (now the library), the Council House and the remains of the Abbey although it is the surrounding gardens with their gravel walks and exotic trees which particularly catches her attention. In these gardens – sadly, long-since gone – she says that the ladies and gentlemen of the town would stroll every Wednesday "as in St. James's Park" and she claims that she saw people of quality "more than in any town except Nottingham". From Shrewsbury she travelled down what is now the A5 alongside the Wrekin and comments that, in spite of local claims that it is the highest hill in England, she has seen others much higher in the north of England. And so out of Shropshire, after passing through the coal mining district, and into Staffordshire.

FITZWARINE, Fulke (12th/13th centuries)

The name of several members of the family during this period, the exploits and actions of whom were attributed to one individual in the Anglo-Norman prose romance **Foulques Fitz-warin.** The work recounts the border settlement of the Fitzwarines and their struggles with neighbouring rivals for power and precedence, in particular over ownership of Whittington Castle which they had built early in the 13th century. While the romance is a mixture of fact and fiction the Fitzwarines certainly did exist and lived at Whittington Castle until 1420 when the male line died out.

FLETCHER, John William (1729-1785)

Evangelical minister and author of religious works; born at Nyon in Switzerland, his real name being Jean Guillaume de la Flechere, of aristocratic descent. After originally intending to follow his father as a professional soldier he attended Geneva University and then came to England in 1752. He was introduced to Thomas Hill of Tern Hall, Atcham and accepted the offer of post of tutor to Hill's two sons. While in London, Fletcher had already met John and Charles Wesley and been impressed by their new Methodist teachings. With the permission of Hill and on the advice of John Wesley he decided upon a career in the Church and was ordained in 1757, having preached his first sermon at Atcham. Although a close friend of John Wesley and although much influenced by Methodism, Fletcher remained within the Church of England. Thomas Hill was the patron of the Madeley living so Fletcher was able to assist the incumbent minister. In doing so he grew to know and love the people of Madeley in spite of their roughness and profanity and, when the living was offered to him in 1760 readily accepted. He in fact devoted the rest of his life to his work among the people of Madeley and surrounding districts. He followed Wesley's practice of founding 'societies' at Madeley Wood and Coalbrookdale and was unstinting in his work for the parish. In spite of initial resistance his parishioners grew to respect and love him. His health began to fail and caused him to leave for a while but he returned as soon as possible.

In 1781 he married Mary Bosanquet from Yorkshire and they founded a Sunday School in Madeley. A frequent visitor to the Madeley vicarage was John Wesley who set out from here to preach in other parts of Shropshire. John Fletcher died at home in August 1785 and was buried beneath a cast iron tomb (appropriately in this birthplace of the iron industry) in Madeley churchyard. His wife survived him by thirty years, continued his work and was buried with him. Their home next to the church still stands although it is no longer the vicarage, but Fletcher's church was replaced in 1796 by a new building designed by Thomas Telford. John Fletcher, whom John Wesley had nominated to succeed him, was of course primarily a preacher but he was also a prolific and nationally known writer whose best known work at the time was **Checks to Antinomianism** (1771).

FORSTER, Edward Morgan (1879-1970)

Novelist, born London and educated at Tonbridge School and King's College, Cambridge. **Howard's End** (1910), one of his most highly acclaimed novels, has major passages set in Shropshire, namely Shrewsbury (" . . . the astonishing city") and Clun. In the novel Forster describes the gathering of the major characters in Shrewsbury at The Raven Hotel (now demolished), having arrived from London via the Great Western Railway. The party leaves by road by means of the Welsh Bridge and travels south through the Shropshire countryside, "conscious of an occasional summit, rounded and wild". Forster provides some excellent passages of description here, particularly the first glimpse of Clun (which he calls Oniton) as the party reaches the summit of the final hill above the town, so that below them they see Oniton " . . . with its church, its radiating houses, its castle, its river-girt peninsula". The novelist has his characters stay at Oniton Grange, a "grey mansion" close to the castle

Clun; E. M. Forster's Oniton.

and in fact a large house called The Villa still stands by the side of the Bishop's Castle road entering Clun and answers to Forster's description — there are rival claimants though. There can be little doubt that Clun is the place Forster had in mind when writing these Shropshire passages in this important novel.

FOX-DAVIES, Arthur Charles (1871-1928)

Heraldic expert and novelist; born in Bristol and educated in London. Fox-Davies wrote two authoritative books on heraldry: **English Heraldry** (1907) and **A Complete Guide to Heraldry** (1909). In addition he was the author of novels and stories (including detective stories) such as **The Dangerous Inheritance** (1907), **The Manleverer Murders** (1907) and **The Duplicate Death** (1910). His parents lived at Paradise, Coalbrookdale from the 1880's onwards and this was presumably his home for much of his life. He died in 1928 and was buried in Coalbrookdale churchyard.

GASKELL, Catherine Milnes (1857-1935)

Writer of light works of fiction such as **Episodes in the Lives of a Shropshire Lass and Lad** (1908) together with pieces about Shropshire; **Spring in a Shropshire Abbey** (1905) for example. After her marriage in 1876 to Gerald Milnes Gaskell she lived at Wenlock Abbey and seems to have made her home a mecca for artistic and literary visitors including the American novelist Henry James (qv) in 1877, 1878 and

Wenlock Priory.

1882 and Thomas and Emma Hardy who signed the visitors' book on August 13th 1893.

GIBBONS, Gavin (1922-1978)

Author and linguist; educated at Shrewsbury School and Queen's College, Oxford and lived in Shropshire from the mid 1950's onwards. Gavin Gibbons wrote on a wide range of subjects — guide books, grammars, local history together with numerous periodical articles and a science fiction novel **By Space Ship to the Moon** (1958). He lived latterly in Meole Brace, Shrewsbury.

GIFFORD, Richard (1725-1807)

Poet; born at Bishop's Castle and gained his degree in theology at Oxford in 1748. He was appointed curate at Richard's Castle in Herefordshire and later became a preacher in Soho. Gifford wrote on miscellaneous subjects together with some poetry.

GOUGH, Richard (1635-1723)

Author of **The Antiquityes and Memoryes of the Parish of Myddle** as the first complete edition of 1875 was called. Gough lived at Newton on the Hill in the parish of Myddle and described himself as a yeoman. His book, which he began in 1700, is not a literary work as such but has become a classic of its kind over the years and is therefore included in this guide. It is in fact a unique and fascinating documentation of a rural community in the Tudor/Stuart period, not just a dry historical account but a very human work full of anecdote, gossip, folklore and a little scandal as well as a valuable amount of factual information. More recent editions of Gough's book have gone under the title **History of Myddle.**

GREVILLE, Fulke (1554-1628)

Poet, dramatist and biographer; educated at Shrewsbury School where he was a contemporary and close friend of Sir Philip Sidney (qv). He wrote a **Life of Sidney** after his friend's untimely death, but it was not published until 1652. Greville was murdered by his own servant in London and his body brought back to his home at Warwick Castle — his ghost is said to haunt his old apartments to this day. Most of his literary works were published posthumously: a collection of poetry and prose in 1633 and **Remains** (1670) together with the **Life of Sidney** mentioned above.

HALL or HALLE, Edward (1499?-1547)

Chronicler; born in London, the son of a Shropshire man, and educated at Eton and Cambridge. He read law at Gray's Inn and embarked upon a career in legal and political spheres. In 1542 he became M.P. for the borough of Bridgnorth. His influential work **The Union of the Noble and Illustre Families of Lancastre and York,** popularly known as **Hall's Chronicle,** was published posthumously by Richard Grafton. While giving a valuable account of the time of Henry VIII, the chronicle glorifies the House of Tudor up to the year 1532. Shakespeare certainly used it as a

Bridgnorth; Low Town from the Castle Walk.

source for some of his earlier history plays. **Hall's Chronicle** was banned by Queen Mary in 1555.

HARRADEN, Beatrice (1864-1936)

Novelist and short story writer; born at Hampstead and educated at Dresden and at Cheltenham, Queen's and Bedford Colleges – she gained her B.A. from London University. Beatrice Harraden was an ardent supporter of female suffrage and she travelled extensively. Her novel **Ships That Pass in the Night** (1893) was a best seller, but she failed to achieve similar success with subsequent books which included novels, short stories and books for children. As a young woman she spent several happy summer holidays lodging at The Green Dragon in Little Stretton, walking and writing. Fond memories of this and of the landlady, a Mrs. Benbow, resulted in her writing a short story called **At the Green Dragon** (1894). Both inn and landlady were affectionately portrayed in this long forgotten story. She received a civil list pension in 1930 and died six years later at Barton-on-Sea, Hampshire.

HAWTHORNE, Nathaniel (1804-1864)

Influential American author, best known for **The Scarlet Letter** (1850) and **The House of the Seven Gables** (1851) as well as volumes of short stories and works for children. He was born at Salem, Massachussetts, of Puritan descent, and educated at

Barracks Passage; Shrewsbury's shuts and passages were admired by Nathaniel Hawthorne.

St Luke's Church, Hodnet; Reginald Heber was rector here.

Bowdoin College, Brunswick, Maine. He was appointed to the Custom House of Salem in 1843 and became American Consul in Liverpool in 1853, remaining there until 1857. It was during this period that he came to Shrewsbury, arriving on the afternoon of 5th September 1855 from Rock Ferry, and stayed at The Lion Hotel on Wyle Cop. Hawthorne was very much taken by the winding streets, the shuts and passages in the town and, especially, by the number and stateliness of the Elizabethan town houses. Although he stayed barely two days he walked a great deal and took an interest in most of the main buildings and streets, remarking that " . . . I never knew such pleasant walking as in old streets like those of Shrewsbury . . . " His memories of this visit can be found in his **English Note-Books** which were not published until 1944.

HAZLITT, William (1778-1830)

Essayist and critic; born at Maidstone the son of a minister and spent several years of his early life with his parents in America. A few months after their return to England in 1787 his father was appointed minister of the chapel in Noble Street, Wem, in Shropshire and William spent the rest of his childhood and youth here. His home, now called Hazlitt House, still stands in Noble Street as a private dwelling. He was educated at private schools and often accompanied his mother and sister to gatherings of ladies in and around Wem, part of the social and pastoral work expected of a minister's family. William was a great admirer of Samuel Taylor Coleridge (qv) and when the poet, about to become a minister himself, preached a probationary sermon at the Unitarian Church in Shrewsbury he walked all the way there in freezing weather to hear him. Hazlitt was bitterly disappointed when Coleridge received an annuity from Josiah Wedgwood, which enabled him to pursue a literary career, for this allowed him to leave Shrewsbury and prevented Hazlitt from making what he had hoped would be a close friendship. Hazlitt at this time was around nineteen years of age and of course, embarking on a literary career himself, was soon to become a friend of the Romantic poets. Among his own best works are **Characters of Shakespeare's Plays** (1817-18), **Lectures on the English Poets** (1818-19) and **The Spirit of the Age** (1825).

HEBER, Reginald (1783-1826)

Poet and hymn writer; born at Malpas, Cheshire (just north of Whitchurch) and educated at Whitchurch Grammar School and Brasenose College, Oxford. He became Rector of Hodnet in 1807 and Bishop of Calcutta in 1822. He is best remembered as a hymn writer: **From Greenland's Icy Mountains** and **Holy, Holy, Holy** are two of the most famous. Heber also wrote verses and a **Narrative of a Journey in India** (1828-44).

HERBERT, Edward (1583-1648)

Philosopher, diplomat, historian and poet; born at Eyton on Severn at the home of Lady Newport (his maternal grandmother) and lived here until the age of nine when he was sent to Denbighshire. He was brought back to Shropshire to study Latin and Greek under a man named Thomas Newton at Diddlebury. Edward stayed there for two years before going up to Oxford in 1596. He led an incident-filled life as a soldier and diplomat (ambassador to France from 1614 to 1624) and was a talented poet, in the style of John Donne. His younger brother George Herbert (not born in Shropshire) is, of course, now considered one of the finest poets of the period. Edward Herbert's **Autobiography** was published by Horace Walpole in 1764 while his poems, in collected form, were not published until 1881. He was the author of philosophical works of which **De Veritate** (1624) is considered the most important and a **Life of Henry VIII** (1649).

HOUSMAN, Alfred Edward (1859-1936)

Classical scholar and poet; born at Valley House, Fockbury near Bromsgrove in Worcestershire and educated at King Edward's School, Bromsgrove and St. John's College, Oxford where, to his shame and humiliation, he failed his final examinations. From 1882 to 1892 he worked at the Patent Office in London and, in his spare time, devoted himself to classical studies and to thereby establish himself as a scholar to regain his pride. He was also writing some poetry during this period but it was his brilliant articles on the classics in scholarly journals which gained him a high reputation and led to his appointment as Professor of Latin at University College, London in 1892. He remained there until 1911 and became a respected and renowned scholar. An apparently rather dry and austere man (at least to those who did not know him well), he astounded his students and colleagues by the publication of his first collection of poems **A Shropshire Lad** (1896), astounded them because of the contrast between the romanticism of the poems and the outward severity of the

"In valley of springs of rivers . . . "

man they knew as their Professor of Latin. **A Shropshire Lad** is a cycle of poems which tells of the central character, Terence Hearsay, who goes to live in London, in exile as it were from his native county. They are very personal, very nostalgic poems with many of Housman's own feelings and emotions contained within them. Of course they are about Shropshire itself, not perhaps the intimately known Shropshire of Mary Webb but, rather, Housman's idealised conception of the county and country life. He uses place-names especially to evoke rusticity, to conjure up nostalgia – it is an idealised view of Shropshire although not without an awareness of some of the harsher realities of life. One of the great ironies about this work, for **A Shropshire Lad** is arguably the county's best known literary testament, is that a number of poems were written before Housman had actually set foot in Shropshire – hence some topographical anomalies. In fact, as a boy he had first seen the distant hills of Shropshire, those " . . . blue remembered hills", from the summit of Worm's Ash Lane near his Fockbury home. It was the memory of this when he himself was in near exile in London which helped to inspire his romantic evocation of Shropshire. When his poems became well known Housman was surprised to find people making literary pilgrimages to see the places he had immortalised. Only then did they discover just how many of the aforementioned topographical anomalies there were. He had visited the county during the period when he was writing the poems, or at least some of them, and used places, scenes and place-names which he had come across. What the literary pilgrims had not bargained for was the fact that he used a fair degree of licence to move places around or to describe one place under another's name if it suited his purpose. So, for example, that well known vane on Hughley steeple in his poem is, in actuality, hard to discover because he had another church in mind – Hughley has no steeple. But of course none of this matters since Housman's poetry does not depend on accurate description of this kind but rather on that marvellous ability to recreate a sense of country life which has passed, if it ever truly existed that is. In 1911 Housman became Kennedy Professor of Latin at Cambridge where his reputation as a classical scholar continued to grow. He wrote further Shropshire poems which were published in his **Last Poems** (1922). Housman died at Cambridge but his ashes were brought to Shropshire and buried near the north door of St. Laurence's Church in Ludlow beneath a tablet bearing some of his own lines:

> Goodnight; ensured release,
> Imperishable peace,
> Have these for yours.

HOW, William Walsham (1823-1897)

Hymn writer and author of sermons and Biblical commentaries; born at College Hill, Shrewsbury, the son of a solicitor, and educated at Shrewsbury School and Wadham College, Oxford. He was appointed curate at Kidderminster in 1846 and two years later took up a similar post at Shrewsbury Abbey which he retained until 1851. He then became rector of Whittington and during this period (twenty-eight years) he wrote the bulk of his published works. Of his many hymns perhaps the most famous is **For All the Saints.** It was only after much persuasion that he left Whittington to become a bishop in the East End of London before moving, in 1888, to the north of England as Bishop of Wakefield. His body was brought back to Whittington for burial.

William Walsham How was Rector of St John the Baptist's Church, Whittington for twenty eight years.

In addition to his literary achievements William Walsham How was responsible for the first public library in Oswestry.

HUGHES, Isaac (1809-1881)

Minor poet; lived and worked in Oswestry as a shoemaker and won second prize in a national poetry competition. Author of one or two collections of verses including **Poems on Various Subjects** (1838) and **Home and Other Poems** (1871).

HULBERT, Charles (1778-1857)

Miscellaneous writer, publisher and editor; born in Manchester. Undertook a career in commerce and in 1803 became co-owner of a cotton factory in Coleham, Shrewsbury. He bought up his partner's shares but in 1804 the factory caught fire and all the stock was lost. Hulbert managed to survive the financial loss, for it was only partially insured, and in the following year married Anna Wood, daughter of Thomas Wood who had founded **The Shrewsbury Chronicle.** Hulbert had always been a religious man and in fact at one stage considered a career in the Church. From the time of his arrival in Shrewsbury he was keen to promote religion to his workers (this of course being at the height of the great evangelical period in this country) and he even set up a factory chapel as well as opening a Sunday School in Coleham in 1807 which proved a great success. In fact the Sunday School was responsible for over six hundred children being taught, or at least helped, to read and write. He became acquainted with the Shropshire Methodist circuit and preached at Wellington, Madeley and Coalbrookdale and assisted Joseph Lancaster in the founding of a school in Shrewsbury. Hulbert had been familiar with printing and publishing processes through his wife's family and in 1814, quite by chance, he purchased a full set of equipment at a Birmingham auction and so set up in the printing business himself. The following year he started **The Salopian Magazine** with many of the literary articles written by himself. However, his cotton business ran into difficulties and he eventually sold out and retired to a new house (called Providence Grove) in Hadnall in 1832. Here he concentrated on his literary projects, which were numerous, and which were often printed in parts and by subscription. His major works include **The History of Salop** (1837) which was the result of twelve years' work, **A Manual of Shropshire Biography** (1839) and his autobiography, **Memoirs of Seventy Years of an Eventful Life** (1852). His later years were marred by personal tragedies, including the premature deaths of two sons and a daughter, and by his own ill health. He died as a result of a stroke in October 1857 and was buried in the family grave at Hadnall.

INGOLDSBY LEGENDS
see
BARHAM, Richard Harris (1788-1845)

IRELAND, John (died 1808)

Author and biographer; born at Trench Farm near Wem where his family were tenants of a Mrs. Shrimpton who was the widow of William Wycherley (qv). She helped Ireland

Charles Hulbert's grave at Hadnall Church.

as a lad, taking charge of his education and arranging for him to become apprenticed to a Shrewsbury watchmaker. He eventually moved to London and worked as a watchmaker for many years. He also got to know many of the literary and artistic personalities of London society and began to collect the engravings of William Hogarth for which he acquired quite a reputation. Ireland was subsequently commissioned by John Boydell (a Shropshire-born printseller) to prepare **Hogarth Illustrated** which was published in two volumes in 1791. A second edition followed in 1793 and in 1798 a third volume was added with a biographical supplement.

JACKSON, Georgina Frederica (1824?-1895)

Folklorist and dialect expert; born at Pulverbatch. Little is known of her early life but she was a keen amateur artist and became a teacher in Chester. Dialect and language were her real interests and she compiled her **Shropshire Word Book** (1879-81) after extensive research and with the assistance of Charlotte S. Burne (qv) and the encouragement of Professor W. W. Skeat (the eminent Anglo-Saxon scholar). The **Shropshire Word Book** is a scholarly and unique work, an extensive glossary of local dialect words and phrases.

JAMES, Henry (1843-1916)

Major American novelist who spent a great deal of time in this country. **English Hours** (1875) recalls his travels to England and includes a chapter on Shropshire — among the places he visited were Stokesay, Ludlow and Much Wenlock. Stokesay Castle made quite an impression on him for he wrote

> I have rarely had . . . the sensation of dropping back personally into the past so straight as while I lay on the grass beside the well in the little sunny court of this small castle and lazily appreciated the still definite details of mediaeval life.

In **The Princess Casamissima** (1886) James refers to and describes a house called Medley Park in Shropshire. Although there is a real place of this name James was more probably describing Condover Hall or Wenlock Abbey where he is known to have stayed in 1877, 1878 and 1882.

JOHNSON, Samuel (1709-1784)

The famous Dr. Johnson passed through Shropshire in July 1774 en route for North Wales and stopped off at Hawkstone where he was shown the splendours of the Park by the daughter of the house (Hawkstone Hall). The good doctor was suitably impressed by what he saw, Grotto Hill and the rest, although he apparently found the walking hard work. In fact he was so impressed that he could not help but compare it with scenes in Derbyshire and proceeded to wax lyrical on the subject:

> It excells Dovedale, by the extent of its prospects, the awfulness of its shades, the horrors of its precipices, the verdures of its hollows and the loftiness of its rocks. The Ideas which it forces upon the mind are the sublime, the dreadful, and the vast. Above, is inaccessible altitude, below, is horrible profundity.

There is no doubt that Hawkstone Park does contain some dramatic scenery but Dr. Johnson does seem to have gone over the top in this description. Could it be perhaps that the combination of a glass of port at luncheon with all that fresh air and exercise had the effect of stimulating the doctor's powers of verbosity? We can only guess.

Stokesay Castle.   _Atcham; grave of Anna Bonus Kingsford._

KINGSFORD, Anna Bonus (1846-1888)

Poet, essayist and editor; born Maryland Point, Stratford, Essex. In 1867 she married Algernon Godfrey Kingsford who was vicar of Atcham. Anna Kingsford was a great feminist who believed that women should have the opportunity to receive higher education. She also supported the movement against vivisection. From 1868 to 1873 she contributed articles for **Penny Post** and in 1872 purchased and edited **The Lady's Own Paper** for a short period. In 1874 she went to Paris to study medicine and gained her M.D. in 1880. She died of consumption in London and was buried at Atcham. Among her published works were a volume of verse **River Reeds** (1866), **Astrology Theologised** (1886), **Dreams and Dream Stories** (1888), **Clothed With the Sun** (1889) and several religious works.

KYNASTON, Francis (1587-1642)

Poet; born at Oteley near Ellesmere and gained degrees at both Oxford and Cambridge. He was called to the Bar in 1611. Kynaston went to the court of Charles I and became the leading figure in a literary group. He wrote a translation of Chaucer's **Troilus and Cressida,** an heroic romance in verse called **Leoline and Sydonis** (1642) and sonnets of high quality.

LANGLAND, William (1331?-1400?)

Poet; possibly born at Cleobury Mortimer, where there is a plaque in the church porch to this effect, although Ledbury and Great Malvern make equally strong claims to his birth. Very little is known of Langland's life apart from information contained in **The Vision Concerning Piers the Plowman.** A lengthy alliterative poem, this is second only in importance to Chaucer's **Canterbury Tales** amongst mediaeval literature.

LARKIN, Philip Arthur (1922-1985)

Poet; born Coventry and educated at the King Henry VIII School, Coventry and St. John's College, Oxford. Generally considered to be one of the finest post-war British

Philip Larkin (second from right) in Wellington Library, 1962 (photo: Shropshire Libraries).

poets, he refused the poet laureateship after the death of Sir John Betjeman (qv) in 1984, perhaps being only too aware of his own failing health. From 1955 he was Librarian of the Brynmoor Jones Library at Hull University, a post which he held with great distinction. After graduation from Oxford in 1943 Philip Larkin spent three years in Shropshire as Librarian at Wellington Public Library, then part of the Urban District Council. It seems that Wellington made an impression on him and certainly the library did, for, in antiquated premises, he had to stoke a reluctant boiler, shelve hundreds of equally antiquated and dust laden books and, virtually single-handed, attempt to bring the service into the twentieth century. During this time he was writing a novel and working on some of his early poems. Three years after he left Wellington it was absorbed by Shropshire County Library and many of the improvements he had advocated were put into practice. In 1962 Wellington Library was enlarged and modernised and Philip Larkin returned to the town where he was still affectionately remembered to formally open the building. He recalled his early introduction to librarianship in Wellington in a witty, nostalgic article in **The Library Association Record,** October 1977.

LAWRENCE, David Herbert (1885-1930)

Novelist and poet; born Eastwood, Nottingham. Lawrence and his German-born wife Frieda returned to Europe from America in December 1923 for a three month stay. In the first week of January 1924 Lawrence travelled to Pontesbury (while Frieda remained in London) to visit his friend Frederick Carter who was a mystic, painter and writer. He stayed for a few days and, during this time, presumably got to explore some of the local countryside including the bleak Stiperstones range topped by the

The Devil's Chair, Stiperstones.

Devil's Chair which had already been an influential symbol and setting for Mary Webb (qv) in her novel **The Golden Arrow** (1916). While in Pontesbury he saw a magnificent bay stallion which provided him with the major symbol for the short novel which ensued. In fact Lawrence's brief stay in Shropshire proved to be one of the few highlights of his time in England for he and Frieda returned to their New Mexico ranch disillusioned at the dreariness of the country and its people. Soon after their return he began to write **St. Mawr** (1925) and in doing so vented his exasperation and anger at the effects of industrialism and, especially, at what he considered to be the parasites of society feeding off it. **St. Mawr** of course is his fictionalised version of the bay stallion he had seen, a typical Lawrence symbol, beautiful, dangerous, full of power and passion. As setting for this story Lawrence used Pontesbury and the Stiperstones for the most significant scenes and indeed the setting is a vital element in the novel. The central scene of this short but intense novel takes place beneath the Devil's Chair when the stallion, with whom Lawrence so obviously sympathises as symbolic of life as it should be, first violently throws the pseudo artist Rico and then kicks the young blond Englishman, Edwards, in the face. One or two Pontesbury people featured in the novel including Frederick Carter as Cartwright. Although Lawrence's stay in Shropshire was only a matter of days it nevertheless led to a most significant literary creation. He is not a writer one would immediately associate with Shropshire but in **St. Mawr** he seems to have sensed and evoked the essence of the place instinctively:

> They came at last, trotting in file along a narrow track between heather, along the saddle of a hill, to where the knot of pale granite suddenly cropped out. It was one of those places where the spirit of aboriginal England still lingers, the old savage England, whose last blood flows still in a few Englishmen, Welshmen, Cornishmen. The rocks, whitish with weather of all the ages, jutted against the blue August sky, heavy with age-moulded roundnesses.

LEE, Ernest George (1896-1985)

Novelist and religious writer; minister at the High Street Unitarian Church in Shrewsbury in the 1930's, during which time he wrote his first novel **The Fleshly Screen** (1937) under the pseudonym Edward Dodge. He had already had short stories published and went on to write, under his own name, books and pamphlets on religious subjects.

LEE, Samuel (1783-1852)

Scholar and Cambridge professor; born at Longnor. Apprenticed to a carpenter but, through his own efforts, taught himself the classics after becoming interested in Latin texts which he had found in the nearby church at Acton Burnell. After losing all his tools in a fire his learning proved invaluable and he became a teacher at Bowdler's Foundation School in Shrewsbury and made the acquaintance of an Oriental scholar. This prompted what was to be a life-long interest in Oriental and other languages. After graduating from Cambridge in 1819 he went on to become Professor of Arabic and later Regius Professor of Hebrew at that university. Among his published works were many translations from the scriptures into Oriental languages, together with commentaries, sermons and essays.

LEIGHTON, William (active 1603-1614)

Poet and composer; lived at Plaish Hall, the family home. Very little is known of his life other than that he wrote a few volumes of poetry and music which included **Vertue Triumphant, or a Lively Description of the Foure Vertues Cardinall** (1603) and **The Teares or Lamentations of a Sorrowfull Soule** (1613).

MACMICHAEL, William (died 1839)

Doctor and author; born in Bridgnorth and educated at Bridgnorth Grammar School and Christ Church, Oxford. After graduation he travelled extensively throughout Europe and into Bulgaria, Turkey and Russia. He became physician to Lord Londonderry, the British Ambassador to Vienna and after returning to take a higher degree at Oxford took the post of Physician Extraordinary to the King. As such he obviously moved in illustrious social circles but he remained a practising doctor throughout his life. In literary terms he was famous as the author of **The Gold-headed Cane** (1827), a unique biographical work recounting the lives and achievements of eminent physicians through the ages. The title was taken from the golden topped cane which, in the early eighteenth century, was the insignia of the physician (at least the wealthy one) and which would have completed the 'uniform' of powdered wig, buckle shoes, silk coat, breeches, etc. Macmichael also wrote biographical essays on Sir Thomas Browne, Thomas Linacre, John Caius and William Harvey and **Lives of British Physicians** (1830).

MAINWARING, Arthur (1668-1712)

Poet, satirist and critic; born at Ightfield in north Shropshire and educated at Shrewsbury School. He was the founder of **The Medley,** an outspoken literary and political periodical and the author of poems and verses, many of them satirical in nature such as **The King of Hearts** (1690).

MASEFIELD, John (1878-1967)

Poet laureate from 1930. Primarily a poet but also wrote novels and stories. Masefield, born at Ledbury in Herefordshire, had family connections in Shropshire – an uncle owned a farm called The Buttery on the Weald Moors near Kinnersley – and he wrote some Shropshire poems, for example in the volume **In Glad Thanksgiving** (1966).

METEYARD, Eliza (1816-1879)

Novelist and children's author; born in Shrewsbury, the daughter of a surgeon. Eliza Meteyard seems to have been a prolific author, her first novel being **Struggles for Fame** (1845). She wrote many stories for children together with a biography of Josiah Wedgwood which was published in 1865. Her subject matter apparently ranged far and wide, from an early prize essay on the subject of **Juvenile Depravity** to later writings on the intriguing theme of extra-mural interment.

MILTON, John (1608-1674)

It is very unlikely that the great poet ever came to Shropshire but he was responsible for one of the county's most important literary events for his **Comus: a Masque presented at Ludlow Castle (1634) before the Earl of Bridgewater, Lord President of Wales** had its first public performance in the Council Chamber of Ludlow Castle. The Earl of Bridgewater was John Egerton who had become President of the Council of the Marches in 1631. His first visit to Ludlow was in July 1634 and he apparently stayed until October. Milton's masque was performed on Michaelmas Night (29th September) and was a grand, formal occasion. **Comus** follows the traditional pattern of the masque, a dramatic entertainment with the emphasis on music, dance and disguise. Milton's rustic scenes in the play are purely imaginary with one or two nominal references to Ludlow included to aid the celebratory nature of the performance. In 1934 there was a major revival of **Comus** at Ludlow Castle involving a cast of hundreds. In post-war years the Ludlow Festival has become an established event and 1984 saw another revival to mark the three hundred and fiftieth anniversary of the first performance of Milton's play.

MONTGOMERY, Bruce (1921-1978)

Novelist and music writer; born in Buckinghamshire and educated at Merchant Taylors' School and Oxford. Towards the end of his university life he began to read detective novels avidly and, in 1944, to write his own. He was now teaching at Shrewsbury School and was in contact with his friend Philip Larkin (qv) who was working at Wellington Library. Montgomery, creator of the professor/detective Gervase Fen, wrote his detective stories under the pseudonym Edmund Crispin. He stayed at Shrewsbury for two years and one of his novels, **Love Lies Bleeding** (1948), is set in a public school which is obviously Shrewsbury. From Shropshire he moved to Abingdon and later to Devon where he wrote music, especially film scores, under his own name.

MOORE, Francis ('Old Moore') (1657-1715)

Physician, astronomer and schoolmaster; born in Bridgnorth, reputedly in one of the cave dwellings in the St. Mary's Steps vicinity. His **Vox Stellarum, an Almanac for 1701 With Astrological Observations** was originally devised as an advertising ploy to help sell his own brand of health pills. Later editions included additional information to the weather predictions of the original publication and of course the name of Moore is perpetuated to this day in the **Old Moore's Almanacs** which are still published. It should be added that the original health pills are, sadly, no longer available!

MOORHOUSE, William Vincent (early 19th century)

Minor poet; lived in Wellington. **The Thresher and Other Poems** (1828) was published by Houlstons of Wellington.

MORTIMER, Mrs. Favell Lee (1802-1878)

Children's writer of religious and educational works; born in London. After religious

Ludlow Castle; the Council Chamber where Milton's Comus was first performed.

51

conversion at the age of twenty-five, she devoted herself to educational work and actually founded several schools herself. Her best known book was **Peep of Day** (1836). She wrote many religious books such as **Line Upon Line** (1837) in which she retold many of the Old Testament stories. She also wrote history and geography books for children and the popular text books, **Reading Without Tears** (1857) and **Latin Without Tears** (1877). In the mid-nineteenth century she lived at Broseley Hall, a large Georgian house close to All Saints' Church in Broseley.

MYRK (or MYRKES), John (15th century)

Poet; a canon of the abbey at Lilleshall. Author of poems, verses and prose pieces reflecting something of the contemporary life of the time.

O'CONNOR, Armel (d. 1955)

Poet; lived at Mary's Meadow, Ludford for some years and was part-time music master at Ludlow Grammar School from 1909 to 1946. Wrote several volumes of verse which were published by Mary's Meadow Press: **The Exalted Valley** (1915), **The Happy Stillness** (1920), **Lilies of His Love** (1920), **The Little Company** (1925) and, in company with Violet O'Connor (qv), **Peacemakers** (1916) which was published by Methuen.

O'CONNOR, Violet (?)

Poet and children's author; wife (?) of Armel O'Connor (qv) and lived at Mary's Meadow, Ludford. She seems to have been a fairly prolific writer of poems, stories and books for children including **The Songs of Mary's Meadow and Other Verses** (1926), **Romantic Ludlow** (1934), **Thoughts For a Working Woman** (1935), etc.

OLD MOORE
see
MOORE, Francis (1657-1715)

ORTON, Job (1717-1783)

Unitarian minister and author of religious works; born in Shrewsbury, the son of a grocer, and educated at Shrewsbury School. He trained for the ministry at Northampton under Dr. Doddridge (the Nonconformist divine and hymn writer) at an academy for the training of dissenting ministers. Orton was appointed minister at the High Street Unitarian Church in Shrewsbury in 1741 and he remained there until his retirement in 1766. He spent his latter years in Kidderminster and died there in 1783. He was buried in Shrewsbury, in the chancel of Old St. Chad's Church. There is a plaque to his memory in the Unitarian Church. Job Orton was one of the founders of and the first Secretary of the Royal Salop Infirmary and was the author of many religious works including sermons, discourses and essays as well as **Memoirs of Doddridge** (1766).

Broseley Hall beyond All Saints' Church; home of Mrs Favell Lee Mortimer.

OWEN, Goronwy (1723-1769?)

Poet; born Anglesey. Became curate of Selattyn, near Oswestry and married Ellen Hughes, daughter of an Oswestry alderman. He obtained the curacy of Uppington in 1748 and, at the same time, was master of the free grammar school in the nearby village of Donnington. During his five years at Uppington he wrote much of his finest poetry, poetry which is highly regarded by scholars of the Welsh language. He left in 1753 for Liverpool and then London before emigrating to Virginia where he was to be the master of a grammar school. Sadly, his wife died during the long voyage and from here on the few details known of his life suggest that it was an unhappy one. He apparently took to drinking and was dismissed from his school for rowdy behaviour. He died in the late 1760's, an impoverished parson.

OWEN, Wilfred (1893-1918)

Poet; born at Plas Wilmot, a large house in Weston Lane, Oswestry, belonging to his maternal grandparents. After their deaths Owen's father, a railway worker, obtained a job in Birkenhead (Wilfred was then four years of age) so the family moved there. In 1907 Mr. Owen was transferred to Shrewsbury and they rented a house, firstly at 1 Cleveland Place and later at 71 Monkmoor Road, a house which they named Mahim (the house has a commemorative plaque to Wilfred Owen). Wilfred, already an aspiring poet, attended Shrewsbury Technical School but was unable to go to university, in spite of passing the London University Matriculation, because of financial restrictions. He taught for a short time at the elementary school on Wyle Cop in Shrewsbury before going to Dunsden in Oxfordshire as lay assistant to the vicar, an appointment which led to him coming close to suffering a nervous breakdown. Then followed a period in France as a private family tutor during which time war broke out with Germany. In 1915 he enlisted in the Artists' Rifles and was later commissioned into the Manchester Regiment. He was posted to France in 1916, the year of the Somme offensive, and endured the awful hardship and horror of life and death in the trenches. These experiences, not surprisingly, changed him dramatically. In fact he changed from a rather effeminate and not entirely likeable youth to a man who cared deeply and unselfishly for the safety and welfare of his fellow soldiers. He had written poetry for some years, some of it quite good, much of it sub-Keatsian in style. Now he began to write with purpose and direction, based on the terrible experiences of the trenches, with a new and far-seeing maturity. He returned to Britain suffering from shell-shock and had the good fortune to become acquainted with Siegfried Sassoon, an accomplished poet and outspoken critic of the war, while recovering at Craiglochart War Hospital in Edinburgh. Sassoon's advice and support gave further impetus to Owen's tremendous literary talent. In a period that measured somewhat less than two years, Wilfred Owen wrote some of the finest and most moving of all poems about war – among his best known pieces are, for example, **Dulce Et Decorum Est, Anthem For Doomed Youth, Strange Meeting** and **The Send Off.** Owen returned to France in August 1918 and was soon involved in heavy fighting in the final offensives of the war. He was awarded the Military Cross but was killed by machine gun fire on November 4th, 1918, just one week before the Armistice, while trying to cross the Sambre Canal with his men. News of his death reached his parents

Plas Wilmot, Oswestry; birthplace of Wilfred Owen.

in Shrewsbury on Armistice Day itself, as church bells were ringing out in celebration. Wilfred Owen was surely Shropshire's greatest writer, one whose words transcend the particular and speak to all people for all time:

FUTILITY

Move him into the sun –
Gently its touch awoke him once,
At home, whispering of fields unsown.
Always it woke him, even in France,
Until this morning and this snow.
If anything might rouse him now
The kind old sun will know.

Think how it wakes the seeds, –
Woke, once, the clays of a cold star.
Are limbs, so dear-achieved, are sides,
Full-nerved – still warm – too hard to stir?
Was it for this the clay grew tall?
– O what made fatuous sunbeams toil
To break earth's sleep at all?

PARKER, Thomas Netherton (died 1848)

Author and philanthropist; lived at Sweeney Hall, Oswestry (he was responsible for the rebuilding of the hall) and was Mayor of Oswestry and a local magistrate. Not strictly speaking a 'literary' writer but his **Leaves Out of the Book of a Country Gentleman** (1847) are perhaps worthy of mention.

PERCY, Thomas (1729-1811)

Scholar, editor and man of letters; born in Bridgnorth in a house at the bottom of the Cartway and educated at Bridgnorth Grammar School and Christ Church, Oxford. He took Holy Orders in 1753. In 1759 Percy married Anne Gutteridge, daughter of a Northamptonshire squire and began his literary career shortly after this with translations from Chinese and Icelandic. In 1765 his great work **Reliques of Ancient English Poetry** was published. This important collection of poetry included forty-five poems drawn from an ancient manuscript which he had rescued from destruction some years before at a friend's house in Shropshire. He added to these many additional poems from manuscripts and other long forgotten sources and so preserved them for posterity. In doing so he acquired a fair degree of fame and, through his dedication of the book to the Duchess of Northumberland (a Percy of course, from an illustrious line) was made tutor to her younger son and Chaplain to the Duke. In 1768 he edited **The Household Book of the Earl of Northumberland in 1512,** a valuable social document. Percy was appointed Chaplain to King George III the following year and, spending eight months of the year in London, became a friend of Dr. Johnson (qv) and Oliver Goldsmith. He was Bishop of Dromore in Ireland from 1782 until his death.

Bishop Percy's House, Bridgnorth.

Morda Lodge; Barbara Pym's Oswestry home.

PHILIPS, Ambrose (c1675-1749)

Poet; born in Shrewsbury, the son of a draper, and baptised in St. Alkmund's Church – educated at Shrewsbury School and St. John's College, Cambridge. After leaving Shrewsbury for Cambridge he spent very little time in Shropshire apart from visits to his mother until her death in 1712. His first poems were published around 1695 but he abandoned an academic career to take a commission in the army. His best known works were his **Pastorals,** the first four of which were published in 1706. Further poems were published alongside those of Pope and received praise from Addison. However, he became somewhat infamous for a quarrel with Pope over the relative merits of their pastorals and was the butt of a great deal of satire on the part of Swift and his friends. In fact Philips was nicknamed Namby-Pamby by them on account of his rather sentimental adulatory verses, written for the children of a nobleman from whom he was hoping to gain patronage. As well as his poems and verses Ambrose Philips was the writer of two tragedies, **The Briton** (1722) and **Humfrey, Duke of Gloucester** (1723).

PITT, Frances (1888-1964)

Naturalist, photographer and writer; born at Oldbury Grange, Bridgnorth. Frances Pitt wrote numerous books and articles on country life and was a highly respected pioneer among wildlife photographers. Her **Country Years** (1961) is a delightful autobiography providing many snippets of Shropshire life from the 1890's onwards with fond memories of local characters, of her own father's hair-raising driving in a Tin Lizzie Ford (all too easily distracted by observations on fields and hedgerows!) and above all of her beloved Shropshire countryside. Frances Pitt lived in Shropshire throughout her life. Her family moved from Oldbury Grange to a nearby farm called Westwood in 1892 and then to The Albyns, three miles south of Bridgnorth, in 1903. She lived here for over fifty years until moving for the last time in 1958 to Castle House, Harley, near Much Wenlock.

PYM, Barbara (1913-1980)

Novelist; born at 72 Willow Street, Oswestry the daughter of a solicitor and educated at Liverpool College, Huyton and St. Hilda's College, Oxford where she read English. She spent most of her childhood at Morda Lodge, a large Edwardian house on the outskirts of Oswestry, which was to remain the Pym family home for many years. Barbara was brought up in a family where the Church played a major part – her mother was assistant organist at the parish church of St. Oswald, her father sang in the choir and there was a longstanding family tradition of having curates home for supper on a Sunday. Both parents were keen members of Oswestry Operatic Society in the 1920's. Barbara's first real creative work (she had been encouraged to write by her mother) was an operetta called **The Magic Diamond** performed by family and friends at Morda Lodge in April 1922. She was writing throughout the 1930's and, indeed, was working on her first novel **Some Tame Gazelle** from 1935 onwards although it was not published until 1950. During the war she joined the W.R.N.S. and after worked for the International African Institute, living with her sister in London. In more recent years and up to the time of her death she was living in a country cottage in Oxfordshire. During the 1950's she gained some success and recognition for novels such as **Excellent Women** (1952), **Jane and Prudence** (1953), **Less Than Angels** (1955) and **A Glass of Blessings** (1958) followed by **No Fond Return of Love** (1961). This last novel seemed to have marked the end of her success for in the next ten or fifteen years she was virtually ignored and out of fashion and, although still writing novels, was unable to get them published. For example, **An Unsuitable Attachment** was written between 1960 and 1965 but did not appear in print until 1982, two years after her death. It was the publication of the superb **Quartet in Autumn** (1977) which heralded her literary rediscovery. Philip Larkin (qv) was a great admirer of her work and it was he who was a prime mover in making this rediscovery possible. She now became a celebrity, in demand at literary events and launches, and her books were reissued. Sadly she died just three years after publication of **Quartet in Autumn** – which had been followed by **The Sweet Dove Died** (1978) – but her popularity has continued and her novels are acclaimed as minor masterpieces of dry humour and poignancy. Three novels were published posthumously: **A Few Green Leaves** (1980), **An Unsuitable Attachment** (mentioned above) and **Crampton Hodnet** (1985).

The Ancient House, Little Stretton; Oliver Sandys moved here in the 1950's.

60

RALPH, Lester (1878-1936)

Novelist; educated at Portsmouth Grammar School and Merton College, Oxford. Lester Ralph was a professional actor for a time, before travelling and living abroad as a teacher, especially in the West Indies. His memories and impressions from this period provided him with the background for his three novels, **Eve of Saba** (1922), **Geoghan's Kid** (1922) and **Hurricane** (1923). **Geoghan's Kid** was in fact selected for presentation to Princess Mary on her wedding in 1922. He had come to Shrewsbury to teach at the Priory School for Boys in 1914 but his work was interrupted by war service. He returned afterwards though and remained in Shrewsbury for the rest of his life, becoming Second Master at the Priory School.

RANDALL, John (1810-1910)

Local historian and publisher; born Madeley. Randall, like a number of others in this guide, is not strictly a literary figure but is included by virtue of his prominence as a writer of books and articles on local subjects, as editor of his own paper and as a local publisher. He began his working life in the china industry, being employed by John Rose and Company of Coalport. Later he set up his own printing office in Madeley and in March 1875 produced the first issue of his Salopian Monthly Illustrated Journal. Among his own published books were **The Severn Valley** (1862), **Handbook to the Severn Valley Railway** (1863), **Old Sports and Sportsmen** (1873), **Clay Industries on the Banks of the Severn** (1877) and his **History of Madeley** (1880) all of which have been reprinted by Shropshire County Library in recent years. John Randall kept the Post Office at 3 Park Avenue, Madeley and died here on 16th November 1910. He was buried at St. Michael's Church, Madeley.

REYNOLDS, John Hamilton (1796-1852)

Poet; born in Shrewsbury and educated at St. Paul's School. Became a clerk with an insurance company but literature was his main interest and, in London, he began to make the acquaintance of a number of well known literary personalities such as Byron, Keats and Leigh Hunt. He was writing poetry at this time and had two volumes published in 1814, a further one in 1816 and **The Garden of Florence and Other Poems** in 1821. His work was sometimes reviewed as being equal to that of Keats but has now sunk into obscurity. He contributed to **The Edinburgh Review** and to **The London Magazine** in the 1820's but after 1825 wrote very little. He had become a solicitor in 1818 and this was presumably a more lucrative career than that of poetry writing. In 1831 he became part-owner of The Athenaeum and seven years later completely ended his literary life by moving to the Isle of Wight as clerk of the County Court where he remained until his death in November 1852.

RICHARDS, Richard (19th century)

Minor poet from Oswestry; schoolmaster who kept schools in Croxon's Square and later Willow Street. His **Wayside Musings: a Book of Poems** was published in 1859.

SANDYS, Oliver (1892-1964)

Novelist; real name Marguerite Florence Jervis. Lived in Wales with her writer husband

Caradoc Evans until his death in 1945. She was the writer of many popular novels of which **Mr Anthony** (1925) and **The Green Caravan** (1922), both of which were made into films, were the best known. In the 1950's she came to live in Little Stretton at The Ancient House and used neighbouring Church Stretton as the setting for her novel **Quaint Place** (1952).

SAVILLE, Leonard Malcolm (1901-1982)

Children's author; born at Hastings, Sussex. Malcolm Saville was a prolific and very popular writer of adventure stories for children the first of which, **Mystery at Witchend** was published in 1943. His stories nearly always have real geographical settings and usually involve a group of bright, alert children solving a mystery or taking part in some kind of adventure. He wrote eighteen Lone Pine adventures which were nearly all set in the Shropshire hills. He first came to Shropshire in 1936, arriving at Church Stretton by train and then continuing by car through Little Stretton, across the level crossing at Marshbrook to the church at Cwm Head and then turning off down winding lanes to a house called Prior's Holt beneath the Longmynd. It was this house together with the valley and hills behind that provided him with the setting for that first story **Mystery at Witchend.** Other stories followed as he discovered the secret places of the Longmynd with successive visits until he widened his settings to include the Stiperstones range further west. These wilder, bleaker hills, scarred by mining waste and broken on the western slopes by deep valleys gave him a different setting for **Seven White Gates** (1944), **Lone Pine Five** (1949) and **The Neglected**

View west over Stiperstones Village to Corndon Hill.

62

Clun Castle; Scott's 'Garde Doleureuse'?

Mountain (1953). Although he never actually came to live in the county Malcolm Saville was a regular visitor to and great lover of Shropshire. On at least two occasions he attended Book Fairs organised by Shropshire Libraries and shared his enthusiasm for books, reading and the places he had written about with scores of visiting schoolchildren.

SCOTT, Walter (1771-1832)

Novelist and poet. Scott's novels, **The Betrothed** and **The Talisman** were published together as **Tales of the Crusaders** (1825). Set in the Welsh Marches, the 'Garde Doleureuse' in **The Betrothed** is based on Clun Castle for he is said to have stayed at The Buffalo Inn in Clun and possibly written part of the novel while he was there.

SHAKESPEARE, William (1564-1616)

Although there is a theory that Shakespeare may have spent some time in Shropshire, possibly at the Eyton on Severn home of the Newport family, this has never been proved conclusively. However, it is known that the dramatist's Company of Actors visited Shrewsbury in 1593, 1603, 1609, 1610 and 1613 and as he often accompanied them on tour it is possible that on at least one occasion he may have visited the county. There are certainly a number of connections with Shropshire of one sort or another contained within some of his plays.

King Henry VI, Part I (1592) is concerned with the wars with France and a leading figure in the play is the great warrior and nobleman John Talbot, Earl of Shrewsbury whom Shakespeare describes as the 'scourge of France'. Talbot was a genuine historical figure who came from Whitchurch and for many years performed heroic deeds for his King and country in battle. Such was his fame in battle that he was known as the 'English Achilles' and it was upon this fame that Shakespeare developed the warrior's character:

. . . Is this the scourge of France?

Is this the Talbot so much feared abroad,

That with his name the mothers still their babes?

Talbot was in his eightieth year in 1453 when he rode into battle for the last time against the French near Castillon with his son alongside him. He was hit in the thigh by shot from a handgun and hacked to death with a battleaxe, his son (who had refused to leave him) suffering the same fate. Talbot's followers afterwards removed their leader's heart and had it buried in St. Alkmund's Church in Whitchurch. It seems that his body was buried at first in France, but later, possibly as many as thirty or forty years later, his bones were carefully exhumed and brought back to Whitchurch for interment. In 1712 St. Alkmund's Church was rebuilt and while clearing the foundations workmen found an urn containing Talbot's heart wrapped in a velvet covering. It was reinterred beneath the church porch and a plaque was erected on the wall to commemorate the man. Inside the church is the tomb and effigy of John Talbot which had been damaged when the original church collapsed in 1711. When the church was rebuilt, the tomb (and bones within it) was replaced as near as possible to its original position. It was not until 1874, when restoration of the tomb was taking place, that a proper examination of the bones was made, thereby confirming that they were those belonging to a well developed and muscular, though aged, man. Examination of the skull showed that death had been caused by a blow or blows from a sharp instrument such as an axe. It seems almost to bring Shakespeare close

Plaque at High Cross, Shrewsbury, relating to the bloody consequences of the Battle of Shrewsbury.

to us, remembering in his play the words of Sir William Lucy, on seeing the bodies of the two Talbots:

> Give me their bodies, that I may bear them hence,
> And give them burial as beseems their worth

and knowing that Sir John Talbot's bones are indeed within St. Alkmund's Church, Whitchurch. There is an interesting, albeit macabre, sequel to this story of the rediscovery of Talbot's bones which Shakespeare's young prince of Denmark might well have contemplated upon had he known of such a fact. That is, that when the bones were found, workmen discovered among them the skeleton of a mouse, and within the skull, a mouse's nest, together with the mummified remains of a further three mice. The **Whitchurch Parish Magazine** in May 1876 provided that very comment which Hamlet might have made, saying that the incident shows us:

> . . . the depth of humiliation to which the mortal body, even of the greatest, is subject during the mysterious interval between the hour of death and the morning of the resurrection.

King Henry IV, Part I (c1597) deals with the rebellion of the Percys, together with Mortimer and Glendower and their defeat by the King and Prince of Wales at Shrewsbury in 1403. The Battle of Shrewsbury is the focal point of the play and includes the death of the rebel, Hotspur, at the hands of the Prince. Just to the north of Shrewsbury is Battlefield and, in the midst of the supposed site of the battle, the collegiate church of St. Mary Magdalene which was founded by Henry IV in honour of those who were slain. Scholars have argued as to whether or not Shakespeare could have visited the site of the battle and whether "yon busky hill" which the King refers to on the morning of the battle was Haughmond Hill – it is an argument which will probably never be resolved. Here, as in many other of his plays, Shakespeare bases his drama on historical fact but is not averse to altering things to suit his dramatic requirements and of course he invents the rogue Falstaff who, in the play, feigns death to escape that actual fate at the hands of the rebel Douglas.

Hamlet (1602): Yorick, the court jester whose skull Hamlet regretfully and philosophically peruses, was almost certainly Richard Tarlton (qv) who was born at Condover. There is a further indirect but interesting link with this play with the so-called Maiden's Garlands, which can be seen in the Shropshire churches of Astley Abbots and Minsterley. These garlands are crown-like hoops, about a foot high, decorated with ribbons, rosettes, paper roses and lilies and they were placed on the coffins of young girls who had died unmarried (especially if they were engaged to be married at the time of their deaths). After the funeral, the garlands were displayed in the church in honour of the dead girls. Today, six or seven of these sad and faded relics can be seen in the church at Minsterley, among the last examples of a custom which died out at the end of the eighteenth century. It seems likely that it was this very custom that Shakespeare had in mind when the priest tells Laertes, after the death of his sister Ophelia:

Yet here she is allow'd her virgin crants,
Her maiden strewments, and the bringing home
Of bell and burial.

Maiden's Garland in Minsterley Church.

SHENSTONE, William (1714-1763)

Poet; lived at Halesowen which, up to the early years of the last century, used to be part of Shropshire. Shenstone wrote pastoral poems of which **The Schoolmistress** (1742) is his best known. A poet of some standing with his contemporaries, including Dr. Johnson (qv), his work is little read today. His published collections include **Poems on Various Occasions** (1737) and **Works in Verse and Prose** (1764).

SHERWOOD, Mary Martha (1775-1851)

Children's author; born near Worcester the daughter of the Rev. George Butt and educated at home and at the Abbey School, Bath (a school which Jane Austen and her sister Cassandra had previously attended). Mary wrote, later in life, that she had had a happy childhood and that her father was very kind to her and yet recalled that from the age of six to thirteen he had forced her to wear a sort of iron collar with back boards over the shoulders to correct a slouch! Perhaps this experience helps to account for the macabre element which runs through her evangelical stories. While in Bath she had attended balls and social events and was considered a society beauty. She had been writing stories from childhood and delighted in reading anything that could spark her imagination. In 1795 her father died suddenly and her life changed drastically. The family moved to Bridgnorth, to a somewhat uncomfortable house in the High Street and Mary now became caught up in fervent religious beliefs, perhaps due partly to her father's death and partly to separation from her beloved cousin Henry Sherwood. Mary and her sister Lucy began to teach at local Sunday schools and to write moral tales for children, which they had published. One of the first of these was Mary's **History of Susan Grey** (1802) which, according to the author, was intended for the instruction of village women and girls. In it, the once innocent young girl, brought up in a Christian manner by her loving parents, faces a downward path to death and damnation through deviation from their example. Her squalid death is ponderously emphasised to show the inevitable fate of all who submit to life's temptations and the author quotes frequently and extensively from the nether reaches of the Bible to prove her point.

This was the first of many such moral tales for children and Mary was probably the most intense and didactic of all the children's writers during the nineteenth century, stressing always the inherent sinfulness of man (and child!). In 1803 she married Henry Sherwood who had returned from army service in the West Indies and she left Bridgnorth. This marked the end of her direct link with Shropshire although an indirect one was maintained by the fact that many of her books were published by Houlston and Son of Market Square in Wellington, a firm of booksellers and printers which was prominent as one of the country's most prolific publishers of evangelical books and broadsheets. In fact Houlstons shop still exists on the same site in Wellington and is now known as Hobsons, selling stationery and fancy goods. Shropshire has a strong evangelical tradition through Baxter (qv), Fletcher (qv) and the visits of Wesley (qv) and the mining and ironworking districts of the Wellington and Coalbrookdale area were a hotbed of religious fervour. Houlstons was well placed therefore to exploit the production of religious books and they published poems and tracts by Patrick Bronte (qv), Mrs. Sherwood herself, her sister Lucy (who became Lucy

Cameron) and many others. Mrs. Sherwood accompanied her husband to India and threw herself into teaching and evangelical work, as well as continuing to write stories such as **Little Henry and His Bearer** (1814) which was to prove one of her most popular works. She returned to England in 1816 and established a school in Worcestershire. In 1818 the first part of her **History of the Fairchild Family** was published, a truly horrific book of moral instruction for children, which well illustrates the author's penchant for the morbid and macabre. Her later writings included **The History of Henry Milner** (1822-37) and **The Lady of the Manor** (1825-29) which consisted of no less than seven volumes of "conversations on the subject of confirmation, intended for the use of the middle and higher ranks of young females". Heady stuff indeed – the lower ranks of young females presumably had to look elsewhere for their moral instruction though. Mrs. Sherwood's fame as an evangelical writer was so great that she was invited to meet William Wilberforce and Elizabeth Fry. However, in the latter part of her career she lost some of her fervour to become a precursor of the Victorian writers of domestic children's tales.

SHORTHOUSE, Joseph Henry (1834-1903)

Minor novelist; born in Birmingham and known chiefly for **John Inglesant** (1881), an historical novel set in the time of Charles I. Lydiard, the large country house described in the opening chapter, is based on Plowden Hall near Lydbury North.

SIDNEY, Philip (1554-1586)

Poet; son of Sir Henry Sidney who was Lord President of the Council of the Marches and whose seat, in this capacity, was Ludlow Castle. Sir Henry was Lord President from 1560 to 1586 but was not in attendance at Ludlow throughout that period. Philip though, would certainly have visited Ludlow as a child and he was sent to Shrewsbury School where he quickly made friends with Fulke Greville (qv). He went on of course to become Sir Philip Sidney, friend of Spenser and one of the most influential of Elizabethan poets. Sidney's life was all too brief but he left literary gems such as **Arcadia** (1590), **Astrophel and Stella** (1591) and the **Apologie for Poetrie** (1591). A statue of Sidney was erected outside the new Shrewsbury School buildings as a memorial to the dead of the First World War.

SIMONS, David (19th century)

Tailor-poet; born in Wales. Apparently came to Shrewsbury in search of a printer and an appreciative audience for his verses. His **Vision of Pengwerne and Other Poems** (1841) was printed by John Davies of High Street, Shrewsbury and proved popular, so his aim was achieved in the first instance. In October 1841 Simons started a weekly sheet called **The Salopian Budget and Border Sentinel.** The first issue was fairly innocuous, albeit wordy, but successive ones became increasingly scurrilous. He was instructed by legal authorities to cease publication but he simply changed the name to **The Salopian Telegraph and Border Review** and continued as before. As a result of the awful slanders which he was devising and printing, Simons, who seems to have displayed a distinct lack of common sense or intelligence, received numerous threats. On one occasion he was accosted by one of his victims and, not surprisingly,

Hobsons, formerly Houlstons, of Wellington; once publishers of evangelical works.

The original Oswestry School.

Caradoc Lodge, All Stretton.

beaten up. On another occasion a gang of men went looking for him with horsewhips – whether they caught up with him is not recorded. He continued with his slanders though and was duly imprisoned for his pains.

SPOONER, William Archibald (1844-1930)

Author and scholar; born in London the son of a barrister and educated at Oswestry School. He won an open scholarship to New College, Oxford and eventually became Warden of New College. He was the author of several books including works on Tacitus, Bishop Butler and William Wykeham but is best remembered for his embarrassing lapses of speech, now known as 'spoonerisms'.

STRETTON, Hesba (1832-1911)

Children's author of great popularity; her real name was Sarah Smith and she was born in Wellington where her father was a bookseller and stationer in New Street. She was educated at a day school for girls run by Mrs. Cranage at the Old Hall in Watling Street and she read widely from among the books in her father's shop. From her mother she inherited deep religious feelings and convictions which were to colour her later writings. She began writing stories when quite young but was twenty-seven years old before she had anything published. Her first success was due in part to her sister Elizabeth who sent Sarah's story **The Lucky Leg** to Charles Dickens (qv) who was then editing **Household Words.** Dickens liked the story, paid Sarah £5 for it and asked for more. She became a regular contributor to the magazine as a result and a friend of

70

Dickens. In 1858 she adopted the pseudonym Hesba Stretton – Hesba was made up from the initial letters of the names of her brothers and sisters while Stretton came from All Stretton which she had visited as a child and where her sister Anne owned a house called Caradoc Lodge. In 1863 Hesba and Elizabeth moved to Manchester then travelled abroad and eventually settled in London. Her most successful and best loved book, **Jessica's First Prayer,** was published in 1867. It first appeared in **Sunday at Home** and was described as " . . . a touching story, simple written, of a girl waif's first awakening to the meaning of religion". In fact over one and a half million copies of the book were sold, a staggering total by any standard, and it was translated into many languages. Hesba Stretton's stories are all very moral, religious pieces which are too mawkish and sentimental for modern tastes but which were very much in tune with the times. In a memoir written for **Sunday at Home** a correspondent commented on the effect of **Jessica's First Prayer** on himself and fellow sailors some years before:

> Every word went right home to our hearts . . . all soft as they were, and I am sure if Miss Hesba Stretton had seen four rough young sailors choking red-eyed over the story . . . she would have been compelled to allow her eyes to overflow with sympathetic joy!

One cannot help but smile at testimonies such as this and wonder if just possibly the sailors concerned were in a maudlin state as a result of too much grog. But for all their moralising and sentimentality, her stories do contain some good characterisation and they did serve the laudable purpose of highlighting the poverty and squalor of the many young waifs and strays among the child population of the Victorian streets. Between 1866 and 1906 Hesba Stretton had fifty volumes published, mostly short religious stories, by the Religious Tract Society. Of her full-length books further best sellers were **Little Meg's Children** (1868) and **Alone in London** (1869). She was appalled at the plight of the country's thousands of impoverished children and, with Baroness Burdett-Coutts, helped to found what was later to become the N.S.P.C.C. From 1870 onwards she and Elizabeth lived in London, moving to their final home, Ivy Croft, Ham, near Richmond in 1890. Hesba died here in October 1911 after a long illness. The church of St. Lawrence in Church Stretton has a memorial window and plaque to Hesba Stretton.

TARLTON, Richard (c1530-1588)

Actor, dramatist and court jester; born at Condover. Tarlton went to London as an actor and was well known in this capacity by the year 1570. He was one of the original twelve members of the Queen's Company of Players. He played the fool on stage and in the audience and was said to have been a favourite of Queen Elizabeth I. In fact his popularity was so great that many inns and taverns bore his likeness on their signs. He was a writer too, with a play to his credit on the popular subject of **The Seven Deadly Sins.** It is thought that Richard Tarlton was the court jester that Shakespeare (qv) had in mind as the original of 'poor Yorick' in **Hamlet.**

TELFORD, Thomas (1757-1834)

Engineer with many Shropshire connections (churches, bridges, roads) and whose name is now commemorated by Telford New Town. Telford also wrote some poetry, for example **To Sir John Malcolm on Receiving His Miscellaneous Poems** (1831). He was also a friend of the poet Richard Southey whom he accompanied on a journey to Scotland – he afterwards wrote an account of their travels.

THYNNE, William (died 1546)

Editor; descended from the Botfield or Boteville family, the Thynnes originated from the now deserted settlement at Caus Castle, near Westbury. They moved to Minsterley and built the Hall which, although much restored, can still be seen near the centre of the village. William Thynne joined the household of King Henry VIII and became Chief Clerk of the Kitchen, a somewhat unlikely sounding occupation for a man of letters. He began to study the works of Chaucer and to collect manuscripts of his poems. His collection grew and he became the leading authority on the subject, eventually publishing the first collected edition of Chaucer's works with notes and commentaries at the press of Thomas Godfrey in 1532. A second edition followed in 1542. Although his editions did contain some spurious pieces, Thynne is important as the first genuine editor of Chaucer.

TWAIN, Mark (1835-1910)

American author and humorist; real name Samuel Langhorn Clemens. Best known for **Tom Sawyer** (1876) and **Huckleberry Finn** (1884). Twain stayed at Condover Hall for a time in 1873, at the invitation of Reginald Cholmondeley. In 1879 he travelled to

Minsterley Hall, once seat of the Thynne family.

The Church of St Eata, Atcham.

Germany, Italy and France, the result of which was **A Tramp Abroad** (1880), and came over to England. He again came to see Cholmondeley and spent a week at Condover, fellow guests on this occasion being the painter Sir John Millais and his wife.

VITALIS, Ordericus (1075-1143?)

Historian and chronicler; born at Atcham and baptised at the church of St. Eata by his godfather, the priest Orderic. He was educated in Shrewsbury from the age of five years and as a young man became a clerk in the church of St. Peter and St. Paul. He left England for France and spent much of the rest of his life at the Norman chapel of St. Evroul. However, he did return to this country to collect material for his great chronicle **Historia Ecclesiastica** (1123-41), a mixture of factual information and gossip about the histories of England and Normandy.

WARD, Mary Augusta (1851-1920)

Novelist; known as a writer always as Mrs. Humphrey Ward. She was born in Tasmania, the daughter of Thomas Arnold (second son of Dr. Arnold of Rugby) and eldest of eight children. When the family returned to England in 1856 Mary was sent to boarding schools. From the ages of ten to fourteen years she attended the Rock Terrace School for Young Ladies in Shifnal, an experience which she evidently did not enjoy. She did however, form a close attachment to the vicar and his wife, the Rev. and Mrs. Cunliffe. She was to recall her Shifnal schooldays in her novel **Marcella** (1894). She married Thomas Humphrey Ward, Fellow and tutor of Brasenose College, Oxford. In 1881 they moved to London where he joined the staff of **The Times** while she contributed articles and reviews. 1884 saw the publication of her first novel **Mrs. Bretherton.** She held a lifelong interest in religion and particularly in the idea of the social functions of religion for the benefit of the poor and weak. Views such as this were embodied in her best selling novel **Robert Elsmere** (1888) and she put her beliefs into practice by founding a settlement for the poor in London which later became the Passmore Edwards Settlement in Tavistock Square. Mrs. Humphrey Ward wrote many more novels in the years leading up to the First World War, combining this with her work for crippled and impoverished children and for women's suffrage. During the war she toured the trenches and wrote up her experiences on behalf of the government for publication in America – these were **England's Effort** (1916), **Towards the Goal** (1917) and **Fields of Victory** (1919). Her autobiography, **A Writer's Reflections** came out in 1918. She died in London and was buried at Aldbury in Hertfordshire.

WEBB, Mary Gladys (1881-1927)

Novelist and poet; born at Leighton Lodge, the eldest child of George Edward Meredith (who taught privately) and his wife Sarah Alice and christened at the nearby church of St. Mary in the grounds of Leighton Hall. The family moved, when Mary was just one year old, to The Grange, a large country house just outside Much Wenlock. Mary spent much of her childhood here and, as she grew older, was taken out for rides in the surrounding countryside by her beloved father from whom she gained much of her knowledge of local places, customs and stories. In 1895, having been educated at home until then, she was sent away to a school in Southport. However, she returned to take charge of the running of the house and the upbringing of her younger brothers and sisters after her mother suffered an injury in a riding accident which left her an invalid for a considerable time. The Merediths moved house again in 1896, this time further away to The Woodlands (now called Harcourt Manor) at Stanton-on-Hine-Heath to the north east of Shrewsbury. The Meredith children now had a governess, Miss Lory, who did much to encourage Mary with her writing and who was to become a lifelong friend. At Stanton, Mary suffered the first breakdown of her health, an attack of nervous illness which developed into Graves' Disease. This was to plague her for the rest of her life and lead to her untimely death. Already a shy

Mary Webb's Birthplace, Leighton Lodge.

75

and sensitive girl, her self consciousness was heightened by the unsightly goitre which was one of the side effects of her complaint. Throughout her childhood and teenage years Mary had loved to walk and cycle in the Shropshire countryside and her early essays published in 1917 as **The Spring of Joy** proved her to have a remarkable eye for and perception of nature in all its manifestations. She also had a great deal of time for the old, the poor and the sick and could talk naturally and easily with them even though tongue tied and shy when in so-called 'polite' society. 1902 saw yet another move, to Maesbrook, a smaller house in Meole Brace, near Shrewsbury. Mary was now reading widely and writing herself as well a taking long walks, especially to Lyth Hill which became her favourite spot. In 1909 her father died and she was distraught. Writing proved something of a therapy and some of her most poignant poems resulted from her loss. She met Henry Webb, a school teacher and distant relative of the ill-fated Captain Webb, and they married in 1912, spending an unhappy two years in Weston-super-Mare where Henry had a teaching job. As Mary was so homesick for Shropshire they returned to rent Rose Cottage in Pontesbury, supplementing their meagre income with the sale of produce from their garden. Pontesbury lies close to the Stiperstones which feature so prominently in her first novel **The Golden Arrow** (1916). Henry took a post in Chester, so they could only return to Pontesbury at weekends (they had moved to a cheaper house at the Nills). Mary's second novel **Gone to Earth** (1917) was the product of this not entirely happy period. In fact she could only be truly happy when living in her beloved Shropshire permanently. They did achieve this by having Spring Cottage built on Lyth Hill – here Mary wrote **The House in Dormer Forest** (1920). By now, after three novels and some enthusiastic reviews, Mary had still not achieved real success or recognition, so she went to London to survey the literary scene and try to widen her audience. Although impressed by some of the literati that she met, this was not a happy time for her and, as usual, she was homesick. Her health was a constant worry with alternate periods of intense nervous activity followed by deep depression. Her marriage too was under stress, due in part to her own possessiveness over Henry. In 1922 she completed her least successful novel **Seven For a Secret** and followed it two years later with what is often considered her best, **Precious Bane** (1924). She did achieve public success with this novel being awarded the prestigious Femina Vie Heureuse prize. By now her health was in rapid decline and her final novel **Armour Wherein He Trusted** (1929) was never completed. She set out to visit her old friend Miss Lory at St. Leonards-on-Sea in October 1927 and died there shortly after arriving. She was buried in Shrewsbury Cemetery. It is ironical that it was only after her death that the public acclaim, for which she had longed, was given to Mary Webb. The then Prime Minister, Stanley Baldwin, praised her work at a literary dinner and this triggered off a remarkable demand for her books, some of which had gone out of print. The novels became best sellers for a number of years up to the outbreak of the Second World War. After the war Mary Webb's name was largely forgotten and only in the last ten years has it begun to emerge and her work be reassessed. Although by no means the finest writer connected with Shropshire, Mary Webb is *the* Shropshire novelist. She loved and knew the county intimately and, in her novels and poems, created from what she saw, perceived and believed that almost timeless landscape within which her characters expend their highly charged emotions and act out their equally

Pontesbury; the former Rose Cottage where Mary Webb wrote The Golden Arrow.

timeless dramas. Most of the towns and villages mentioned in her novels under fictitious names are easily identifiable. For example 'Silverton' is Shrewsbury, 'Mallard's Keep' is Bishop's Castle, 'Slepe' is Ratlinghope and so on. For those who wish to find out more about this talented but rather sad Shropshire writer the following biographies are thoroughly recommended: **Goodbye to Morning** (1964) by Dorothy P. H. Wrenn and **The Flower of Light** (1978), a scholarly and substantial work, by Gladys Mary Coles who has done much to revive the name and reputation of Mary Webb. The compiler of this **Literary Guide to Shropshire** has written a booklet on Mary Webb which may also be found useful: **Mary Webb. A Narrative Bibliography of Her Life and Work** (1981).

Bromlow Callow in the heart of the Mary Webb country.

WESLEY, John (1703-1791)

Methodist preacher and leader, hymn writer and author; educated at Charterhouse and Christ Church College, Oxford. In the 1730's he began to preach and undertook extensive tours throughout Britain, often suffering abuse and physical hardship but persevering regardless. For the remainder of his life he travelled thousands of miles on horseback and is estimated to have preached over forty thousand sermons. As a writer he had twenty three collections of hymns published (1737-86) together with

Wesley House, Fish Street, Shrewsbury.   *Ironbridge seen and admired by John Wesley.*

collected prose works (1771-74). The standard edition of his **Journal,** a fascinating and moving work, was published between 1909 and 1911. Wesley was a friend of John Fletcher (qv) and became a regular visitor to his Madeley vicarage. In fact Fletcher's ministry in Madeley was everything that Wesley had envisaged for Methodism; that is, the process and practice of Methodism *within* the Church rather than at odds with it. John Wesley spent much of his time and efforts among the working people of the Black Country but would often think nothing of riding the forty or fifty miles to Shrewsbury where he would stay at the home of a Mrs. Glynne in Dogpole. On his first visit to the town in March 1761, he preached at 1 Fish Street (a building now known as Wesley House). Over a period of time he came into contact with many of the town's most prominent people and it was on one of these visits that he was invited to preach in the Anglican chapel in the grounds of Berwick House, just outside Shrewsbury on the road to Baschurch. A year after his first visit Wesley travelled from Hereford to Shrewsbury in appalling weather conditions – snow, rain, the road barely passable – and recalled that, at Church Stretton, one of the horses lay down and refused to go further. He made it though and a day or two later moved on to Wem, again a difficult journey in snow and mud, to preach to a small congregation in the Market House. In July 1764 he came to Madeley and after Fletcher had read the prayers he preached to a vast congregation. The congregation was so great that many could not get into the church so a window was removed to allow those outside to hear. Some years later, in July 1773 Wesley arrived at Madeley from Liverpool and the following morning (10th July) went to Buildwas to see for himself the effects of the earthquake which had occurred the previous month and which had created great chasms and mounds and even changed the course of the River Severn. Just over twelve months later on Saturday 30th July 1774 Wesley preached from beneath a sycamore tree in Madeley Wood to a large congregation of colliers who, he said, ". . . drank in every word". The following morning and afternoon he again had large congregations in Madeley but these were surpassed by that which awaited him that evening across the river in Broseley. He was again in Shropshire in May 1779, preaching in the new chapel at Madeley Wood and in Shrewsbury on the 25th and, the following day, in the Assembly Rooms at Broseley. Afterwards he walked to Ironbridge to see the first, magnificent cast iron bridge nearing completion. In April 1781 he viewed the bridge once more, remarking that it was ". . . the first and the only one in Europe. It will not soon be imitated". From this brief account of some of Wesley's visits to Shropshire it will be seen that his presence was a significant one. But it is hardly surprising that he should have come so often, since the man he had singled out as his successor, John Fletcher, had chosen the mining town of Madeley in which to conduct his ministry and to devote the rest of his life to the colliers and ironworkers and their families. Fletcher had no ambition to succeed Wesley and, in the event, died before him. The work of Fletcher, Wesley and other preachers of their persuasion in the industrial districts of Shropshire is often forgotten today. Their relevance in a literary gazeteer such as this may be slight but their overall significance was great indeed and it is surely not too fanciful to suggest that they must have indirectly influenced those two early children's writers, Mrs. Sherwood (qv) and Hesba Stretton (qv).

WEYMAN, Stanley John (1855-1928)

Novelist; born at 54 Broad Street, Ludlow, the son of a solicitor and educated at Ludlow Grammar School, Shrewsbury School and Christ Church College, Oxford. He began writing in a minor way while at Oxford, where he read history, and increased his output in the following years with articles for **The Cornhill Magazine.** He in fact spent ten years as a barrister before turning to a literary career full time, due largely to the influence of the magazine's editor. Weyman travelled abroad and his experiences and observations provided him with much of the background for the historical stories and romances for which he became well known. On one occasion he was arrested under suspicion of being a spy in the south of France and was only released after the intervention of the British Ambassador. His novels include **Memoirs of a Minister of France** (1895), **The Red Cockade** (1895), **The Long Night** (1903), **The Wild Geese** (1908) as well as many short stories. **The Wild Geese** was to have been his last novel but, some years later he added **The Great House** (1919) and **Ovington's Bank** (1922), both of which were published in serialised form in **The Cornhill Magazine.** Weyman's novels are only rarely read today although **Under the Red Robe** (1894) is sometimes remembered. **The New Rector** (1891),

Broad Street, Ludlow.

although supposed to be set in Warwickshire, actually contains passages describing Ludlow and South Shropshire. He lived in Ludlow until the late 1890's after which he moved to Ruthin in North Wales where he spent the remainder of his life and where there is a statue in his memory.

WILLIAMS, John Bickerton (1792-1855)

Minor poet and nonconformist writer; born at West Felton. Practised as a solicitor in Shrewsbury for many years and became Mayor in 1836. On retirement lived at The Hall, Wem.

WILLIAMS, Robert (1810-1881)

Antiquarian, biographer and linguist; born at Conway and educated at Shrewsbury School and Oxford. From 1838 to 1879 he was curate of Rhydycroesau, near Oswestry and from 1879 to his death, rector of Culmington near Ludlow. Robert Williams was the author of a number of antiquarian studies together with two significant works of Celtic scholarship, **Enwogion Cymru: a Biographical Dictionary of Eminent Welshmen** (1852) and **Lecicon Cornu- Britannicum: a Dictionary of the Ancient Celtic Language of Cornwall** (1865).

WODEHOUSE, Pelham Grenville (1881-1975)

A prolific and extremely popular writer of humorous novels. Wodehouse was the son of a Hong Kong civil servant, who retired through ill health and returned to England, firstly to Dulwich and then to Hay's House, Stableford in Shropshire. Young P. G. Wodehouse, although educated away from home at boarding school, returned to Stableford for his holidays and grew to know the district well between the ages of fourteen and twenty one (when the family moved again to Cheltenham). He retained a great affection for the county, particularly the area around Stableford, which is a few miles from Bridgnorth, and it was to become one of the major sources for composite settings in the novels, together with Gloucestershire, Worcestershire and Wiltshire. Wodehouse's last, unfinished novel was **Sunset at Blandings** which Richard Usborne edited in 1978 after the author's death. Usborne followed up all references to Shropshire in the various Wodehouse novels, but especially this last one, and consulted contemporary railway timetables to see if fictional journeys could actually have been made. All this was in an effort to identify and locate the original of Blandings Castle. Usborne's conclusion was that it must be Buildwas, a mile or so up the Severn from Ironbridge. However, since Usborne's conclusions were published N. T. P. Murphy has come up with a different theory in his fascinating book **In Search of Blandings** (1981). He concludes, having closely examined all the novels and visited dozens of locations, that Blandings Castle was situated at Weston Park on the Shropshire/Staffordshire border. He qualifies this though, by saying that the actual castle, in his opinion, is Sudeley Castle in Gloucestershire, but that the setting of Blandings is based on Weston Park (most of which is in Staffordshire although a section of the park is in Shropshire). His arguments are certainly convincing as he takes us through the other possible locations, such as Morville and Aldenham Hall, and dismisses them. Murphy concedes that Aldenham Hall, with its famous iron gates, was very much in Wodehouse's mind when describing his fictional Matchingham Hall. In the Blandings novels there is much coming and going by train from Market Blandings and Murphy therefore suggests that the small town of Shifnal, on the main railway line from London, fits the bill perfectly. Of course, the identification of fictional locations is always open to conjecture since writers so often use artistic licence, to say nothing of composite settings. There is little doubt that Wodehouse did know this corner of Shropshire well, so that his fictional Worbury is very likely based on Worfield, Eckleton on the real Ackleton and Bridgeford on Bridgnorth. And it must be more than coincidence that Wodehouse refers to a spot called Badgwick Dingle when a glance at the map shows us that, not far from Stableford, there is Badger Dingle. Richard Usborne to some extent and N. T. P. Murphy especially, have apparently covered much of the ground in locating the Shropshire connections in the novels of P. G. Wodehouse. Perhaps future investigators of this perennially popular writer's books will come up with further locations and theories – already there seems to be plenty of scope for Wodehouse pilgrimages on the Shropshire/Staffordshire border.

Stableford; Hay's House where young P. G. Wodehouse spent summer holidays.

WRIGHT, Thomas (1810-1877)

Antiquarian and biographer; born at Tenbury and educated at Ludlow Grammar School and Trinity College, Cambridge. He moved to London in 1836 and adopted writing as a profession with archaeology, history and biography being his favoured subjects. He was the author of over eighty works including **Queen Elizabeth and Her Times** (1938), **Biographia Britannica Literaria** (1842-46), **The Celt, the Roman, and the Saxon** (1852) and **The History of Domestic Manners and Sentiments in England During the Middle Ages** (1862). He was superintendent of excavation at Wroxeter in 1859, was a Fellow of the Society of Antiquaries and held office in the Camden, Percy and Shakespeare Societies.

WYCHERLEY, William (1640-1716)

Dramatist; born at Clive Hall, near Wem of a long established Shropshire family. His father was said to have appropriated public money for his own use and to have bought the manors of Wem and Loppington, fending off the resulting lawsuits in the process. William spent much of his childhood at another of the family's properties,

Clive Hall; birthplace of William Wycherley.

84

Trench Farm, between Clive and Wem. He was educated in France and at Oxford but spent most of his life in London, where he displayed a marked preference for the taverns and bawdy houses of the seedier parts of the capital. His plays, mostly satirical and sometimes savagely so, include **Love In a Wood, or St. James's Park** (1672), **The Gentleman Dancing Master** (1673), **The Plain Dealer** (1674) and **The Country Wife** (1675). After publication of his **Miscellany Poems** in 1704 he gained the friendship of Pope, who went on to revise and edit many of his writings. Wycherley was forced to return to his father's house in Clive in 1689 to take refuge from a potentially dangerous political scene – William III was not one to favour literary men, certainly not libertines such as he. Wycherley must have been desperate to escape, for he hated country life and country people and the watchful presence of his disapproving father would have sorely tried him. However, he managed to break his Shropshire exile from time to time by means of short periods back in London. In Shropshire, apart from feuding with his father over his many debts, he spent his time corresponding with old friends in London and writing poetry. His father bargained with him over the terms of his will. William was to receive only a small amount of the family estate but his father agreed to pay off £1,000 of his debts – the errant son readily agreed to this arrangement and returned to London. The old man died in May 1697 and was buried beneath the chancel of All Saints' Church, Clive. William, whose first wife had died many years before, decided very late on in life to remarry in order to rid himself of further debts. A cousin of his, Captain Thomas Shrimpton, told him he could find him a rich bride who would fit the bill perfectly. He duly arrived with one Elizabeth Jackson, a coarse and unrefined woman who was said to be Shrimpton's mistress. After some delay William, now an old man and in his dotage, married the woman and his debts were discharged. He just had time to make over Trench Farm to her before he died on 31st December 1716. So ended the rumbustious life of 'manly Wycherley' as he was called.

YOUNG, Francis Brett (1884-1954)

Novelist; born at The Laurels, Halesowen, Worcestershire and educated at Epsom College and Birmingham University where he studied medicine. He discovered and grew to love the Welsh borderland early on in life and called upon memories of the area for settings in many of his novels, for example in **The Dark Tower** (1914), **The Crescent Moon** (1918) and **The House Under the Water** (1932). He was not a Shropshire novelist as such but his frequent descriptions of the Marches include the county, with which he was certainly familiar, and his novel **The Iron Age** (1916) is set partly in Ludlow.

Atcham; The Old Bridge.

PART 2: PLACES

ALDENHAM HALL

Fine country residence with magnificent wrought iron entrance gates, close to the village of Morville on the A458 and approximately 3½ miles NW. of Bridgnorth. Probably the original of the fictional Matchingham Hall in some of the Blandings stories of P. G. Wodehouse (1881-1975).

ALL STRETTON

Village on the B4370, 12 miles SSW. of Shrewsbury. Hesba Stretton (1832-1911) often spent time here visiting her younger sister, Ann, who lived at a house called Caradoc Lodge. Hesba eventually took the name 'Stretton' as part of her nom de plume when she became a writer.

ATCHAM

Village on the A5, 4 miles SE. of Shrewsbury. There are most attractive views here with the church of St. Eata standing on the banks of the Severn, the Georgian Mytton and Mermaid Hotel and the original Severn Bridge flanked by its more recent successor. Across the road are the entrance gates to Attingham Hall, the finest country house in the county which incorporated the former Tern Hall. Anna Bonus Kingsford (1846-1888) came to live in Atcham after her marriage to the vicar. One of the handful of mediaeval writers linked with the county, Ordericus Vitalis (1075-1143?), was born in Atcham and baptised at the church of St. Eata — a church with a unique dedication and long architectural history.

BADGER

Pretty, picture-postcard village in the east of the county, on a minor road, approximately 6 miles NNE. of Bridgnorth. Isaac Hawkins Browne (1705-1760), the poet and M.P., lived here as did his son of the same name. Badger is one of a number of villages in the district which P. G. Wodehouse (1881-1975) knew well from his teenage years and which figure in some of his stories. Badger Dingle, a delightful walk through the grounds of the Hall (demolished some years ago), appears in fictionalised form as Badgwick Dingle.

BATTLEFIELD

Site of the Battle of Shrewsbury in 1403, lying just off the A49, 3 miles NE. of Shrewsbury. The church of St. Mary Magdalene, well worth a visit for its own sake, was founded by King Henry IV in honour of the dead in the battle. The whole site has a great sense of atmosphere, particularly at dusk, and it is not too difficult to imagine oneself back in time, perhaps viewing the aftermath of the conflict when the rebels, with Hotspur to the fore, were routed by the King and his followers. Not too difficult also to imagine Shakespeare's version of the events, with Falstaff feigning death to save his skin and the Prince and Hotspur in bloody combat, for this battle forms the climax to **King Henry IV Part 1.** One of Shropshire's most successful authors, Edith Pargeter, has set her novel **A Bloody Field by Shrewsbury** (1972) here as well.

BECKBURY
Village on minor road, approximately 4½ miles SE. of Shifnal. Wilfred Byford-Jones (1907-1977) lived at Lower Hall before retiring to Machynlleth.

BISHOP'S CASTLE
Small and ancient town just off the A488, 18 miles SW. of Shrewsbury. The birthplace of Richard Gifford (1725-1807) and called Mallard's Keep in the novels of Mary Webb (1881-1927).

BOMERE POOL
Large, natural pool lying to the E. of the A49, between Bayston Hill and Condover,

Saint Mary Magdalene, Battlefield.

88

Bishop's Castle; The House on Stilts.

about 4 miles S. of Shrewsbury. Mary Webb (1881-1927) used to spend much of her time at this once-secluded spot which is almost certainly the original of her Sarn Mere in **Precious Bane** (1924). If the spirit of the novelist still haunts the spot it is presumably horrified at the present use made of the pool for it is now regularly used for water-skiing.

BRIDGNORTH

Ancient and spectacular town on the Severn, standing at the junction of the A442, A454 and A458, 22 miles SE. of Shrewsbury.

Richard Baxter (1615-1691) was an assistant minister at St. Leonard's Church in 1640 and lived in a tiny half-timbered cottage in the delightful church close.

Robert William Eyton (1815-1881) was educated at Bridgnorth Grammar School.

Edward Hall or Halle (1499?-1547) was M.P. for the town in 1542.

William MacMichael (died 1839) was born in the town and educated at the Grammar School.

Francis Moore (1657-1715) of **Old Moore's Almanac** fame was thought to have been born in one of Bridgnorth's many cave dwellings, possibly near St. Mary's Steps.

Bridgnorth Castle.　　　　　　　　　*One of Bridgnorth's many cave dwellings.*

Thomas Percy (1729-1811) was born in what is now the oldest house in Bridgnorth at the bottom of the Cartway and was educated at the Grammar School.

Frances Pitt (1884-1964), the naturalist, writer and photographer, was born at Oldbury Grange.

Mary Martha Sherwood (1775-1851), prolific author of moral tales for children, lived at a house in the High Street from 1795 until her marriage in 1803.

BROSELEY

Small town in the heart of the clay and iron-working district of the Severn Gorge on the B4373 and B4375, 6 miles NW. of Bridgnorth. Broseley stands outside the Telford New Town area and has remained largely unchanged for many years. Shropshire has quite a collection of nineteenth century children's writers associated with it and one of them, Mrs. Favell Lee Mortimer (1802-1878), lived here for a time at Broseley Hall. John Wesley (1703-1792) preached in the town on several occasions to large and enthusiastic congregations.

BUILDWAS

Village on the B4380 and B4378, 3½ miles NNE. of Much Wenlock. On the Much Wenlock side of the River Severn stand the picturesque and dignified ruins of Buildwas Abbey. Buildwas Park is a possible location of the fictional Blandings Castle in the novels of P. G. Wodehouse (1881-1975) although Weston Park (qv) now seems a more likely candidate.

CASTLE PULVERBATCH

Village on minor road which runs between the Longmynd and Stiperstones ranges, approximately 8 miles SW. of Shrewsbury and 4 miles SE. of Minsterley. The village was once fortified by a Norman castle but all that remains now is the grass and scrub-covered motte. Mary Webb (1881-1927) called the place Polrebec in her last, unfinished novel **Armour Wherein He Trusted** (1926).

CAUS CASTLE

Deserted castle and township at the east end of Long Mountain, near Westbury. The overgrown site now appears as a series of ditches leading up to a most impressive motte with just a few remnants of masonry being all that is left of the castle which was reported as being in decay by the year 1521. It overlooks the B4386 Shrewsbury to Montgomery road and is about 2 miles SW. of Westbury. The Thynne family originated from Caus Castle but moved to Minsterley in the early 17th century. William Thynne (died 1546), first editor of Chaucer's works, may well have been born at Caus.

CHURCH STRETTON

Small town beneath the Longmynd on the A49, 13 miles SSE. of Shrewsbury. Once a small village, Church Stretton expanded greatly in the late Victorian and Edwardian period when it became a popular health resort.

Caus Castle, one of the county's many lost townships.

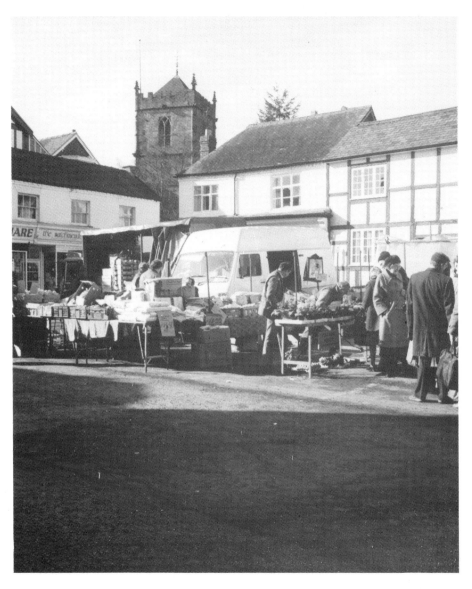

Market Day in Church Stretton.

E. M. Almedingen (1898-1971), the biographer and children's writer, lived here in the 1930's.

Oliver Sandys (1892-1964) lived nearby in Little Stretton (qv) and set her novel **Quaint Place** (1952) in Church Stretton.

Hesba Stretton (1832-1911) came here often before moving away from Shropshire when she became an established author. There is a plaque to her memory in St. Lawrence's Church together with a window depicting the figure of Jessica from her immensely popular story **Jessica's First Prayer** (1866).

Mary Webb (1881-1927) called the town Shepwardine in her novels, particularly in **The Golden Arrow** (1916).

CLEOBURY MORTIMER

Small town on the A4117, 12 miles E. of Ludlow, notable for its church with crooked spire. Simon Evans (1895-1940) came to live here after the First World War and used Cleobury Mortimer and the surrounding area in his stories. William Langland (1331?-1400) was possibly born here – the church has a plaque and memorial window to the author of **Piers Plowman.**

CLIVE

Village lying at the W. end of Grinshill Hill on a minor road off the A49, 3 miles S. of Wem. The dramatist William Wycherley (1640-1716) was born here at Clive Hall.

CLUN

Small town on the A488 and B4368, 29 miles SW. of Shrewsbury and 8 miles W. of Craven Arms. Clun is dominated by the romantic ruins of its Norman castle and by its Norman church with massive fortress-like tower. E. M. Forster (1879-1970) called the town Oniton in **Howard's End** (1910) and Sir Walter Scott (1771-1832) is thought to have been describing Clun Castle when he wrote his **Tales of the Crusaders** (1825) and referred to the Garde Doleureuse.

COALBROOKDALE

Village at the centre of the ironworking district and often said to be the birthplace of the Industrial Revolution. Coalbrookdale lies on the B4373, 5 miles S. of Wellington. The novelist and heraldic expert Arthur Charles Fox-Davies (1871-1928) lived at Paradise, Coalbrookdale and was buried at Holy Trinity Parish Church.

CONDOVER

Village on a minor road off the A49, 4½ miles S. of Shrewsbury. Condover Hall is a magnificent Elizabethan house, now a school for the blind, which used to belong to the Cholmondeley family in the last century. Mary Cholmondeley (1859-1925) lived here for a few months in 1896 before moving to London. Her uncle, Reginald Cholmondeley owned the house before this and was host to the American writer Mark Twain (1835-1910) when he visited in 1873 and 1879. The village of Condover was the birthplace of Richard Tarlton (c1530-1588), actor, court jester and thought to be the original of Shakespeare's 'poor Yorick'.

Clun's ancient Church of Saint George.

CRAVEN ARMS

Village on the A49, famous for its sheep fairs, 7 miles S. of Church Stretton. Called The Junction in the novels of Mary Webb (1881-1927).

CULMINGTON

Village on the B4365, 5 miles NW. of Ludlow. The author and artist Richard Duppa (1770-1831) lived in the village while the linguist Robert Williams (1810-1881) was rector from 1879.

DIDDLEBURY

Village just off the B4368, 7 miles N. of Ludlow. As a boy Edward Herbert lived here from 1594 to 1596 while studying the classics under one Thomas Newton.

DONNINGTON

Village just off the B4380, 8 miles SE. of Shrewsbury. Richard Allestree (1619-1681) and Richard Baxter (1615-1691) both attended the free grammar school in the village – Baxter later taught here for a short time. The Welsh writer Goronwy Owen (1723-1769?) was master of this school and lived in the village.

EATON CONSTANTINE

Village just off the B4380, 10 miles SE. of Shrewsbury. Richard Baxter (1615-1691) lived here from the age of ten years. His childhood home, now called Baxter's House (a private residence), is the 16th century timber-framed house in the centre of the village.

EDGMOND

Village on the B5062, 3 miles W. of Newport. The poet Richard Barnfield (1574-1627) was brought up in the village and Charlotte Burne (1850-1923), the great folklorist, lived here.

EYTON ON SEVERN

Village off the B4380, 8 miles SSE. of Shrewsbury. All that remains of the former mansion house, home of the Newport family, is a most impressive tower (said to be a summer house) set into the wall of the former garden. The poet, philosopher and diplomat Edward Herbert (1583-1648) was born here and spent the first nine years of his life in Eyton.

HABBERLEY

Small village lying in a hollow in the hills, between Pontesford Hill and the Stiperstones, on a minor road 9½ miles SW. of Shrewsbury. There is an attractive grouping of old cottages, farm buildings, church and seventeenth century manor house which is surely little changed from Mary Webb's time. She called the place and surrounding district Bitterley in her novel **The Golden Arrow** (1916).

The Old Summer House at Eyton on Severn.

The Old Rectory, Hodnet, where Mary Chol-mondeley was born in 1859.

The Church of Saint John the Baptist, Hughley.

HADNALL

Village on the A49, 5 miles NNE. of Shrewsbury. Charles Hulbert (1778-1857) the businessman and writer retired to a house called Providence Grove in the village and was buried close to the gate of the churchyard of St. Mary Magdalene.

HALESOWEN

Town on the River Stour, 7 miles W. of Birmingham and not in Shropshire at all. However, in the early years of the last century Halesowen was situated in an 'island' of Shropshire in the midst of the industrial West Midlands and is therefore included in this guide. William Shenstone (1714-1763), the minor poet, lived in the town and Francis Brett Young (1884-1954) was born at The Laurels.

HARLEY

Village just off the A458 with glorious views of Wenlock Edge, 10 miles SE. of

Shrewsbury. Frances Pitt (1888-1964), the well known writer and naturalist, lived latterly at Castle House.

HAUGHMOND ABBEY

The beautiful ruins of the abbey, which was founded in the twelfth century, lie on the lower slopes of Haughmond Hill on the B5062, 3 miles NE. of Shrewsbury. John Audelay (early 15th century) was a poet and canon of the abbey.

HAWKSTONE

Hawkstone Park lies between the A49 and A442, approximately 13 miles NNE. of Shrewsbury. Samuel Johnson (1709-1784) visited Hawkstone on one of his tours and was lavish in his praise of the house and, especially, the park with its caves, precipices and grottos. Hawkstone is also claimed to be the setting for an Arthurian poem, **Sir Lancelot and Sir Turquine,** which is included in **The Reliques of Ancient English Poetry** collected by Thomas Percy (1729-1811).

HODNET

Village on the A53 and A442, approximately 12 miles NE. of Shrewsbury. Another most attractive village with many half-timbered houses and an ancient church with unusual octagonal tower. The novelist Mary Cholmondeley (1859-1925) was born at what is now The Old Rectory across the road from St. Luke's Church and spent the first thirty years or so of her life in this North Shropshire village. In fact this house was built for Reginald Heber (1783-1826), the poet and hymn writer, who was then rector but later became Bishop of Calcutta.

HUGHLEY

Village on a minor road beneath Wenlock Edge, 5 miles SE. of Much Wenlock. The village and the church particularly were immortalised by A. E. Housman (1859-1936) in **A Shropshire Lad** (1896). The church of St. John the Baptist may not have the steeple that Housman refers to but it does have a beautifully carved screen and some ancient stained glass by way of compensation.

IGHTFIELD

North Shropshire village on a minor road off the A41, 4 miles SE. of Whitchurch. The poet and editor Arthur Mainwaring (1668-1712) was born here.

KENLEY

Village on a minor road off the A458, 7 miles W. of Much Wenlock. Archibald Alison (1757-1839) was rector here in this quiet and isolated village where there are delightful views across the Shropshire hills.

LEIGHTON

Village on the B4380, 9 miles SE. of Shrewsbury. Mary Webb (1881-1927) was born at Leighton Lodge.

LILLESHALL ABBEY

The ruins of the twelfth century abbey lie just off the A518, 3 miles SW. of Newport. John Myrk (15th century) was a canon of Lilleshall Abbey and minor devotional poet.

LITTLE STRETTON

Village on the B4370, 1½ miles SW. of Church Stretton. The novelist and story writer Beatrice Harraden (1864-1936) used to stay at The Green Dragon, one of two inns in the village, and depicted it in one of her stories. The best selling novelist Oliver Sandys (1892-1964) lived latterly at The Ancient House across the road from the thatched, half-timbered church.

LONGMYND

Upland plateau cut into by a succession of deep and very beautiful valleys. The Longmynd is about 6 miles in length and extends from Plowden in the SW. to Ratlinghope in the NE. Malcolm Saville (1901-1982) used it as the setting for many of his children's stories while Mary Webb (1881-1927) gave it the fictitious name of the Wilderhope range in **The Golden Arrow** (1916).

LONGNOR

Village on a minor road just off the A49, 8 miles S. of Shrewsbury. The great linguist Samuel Lee (1783-1852) was born there.

View of the Long Mynd from the Caradoc.

LUDFORD

Delightful and secluded village across the Teme from Ludlow and connected with the town by the mediaeval Ludford Bridge. Armel O'Connor (d. 1955) and his wife Violet lived in the parish of Mary's Meadow where they wrote their Christian poems and set up their own press.

LUDLOW

Ludlow's architectural and scenic delights have been extolled in just about every guide book written about the county. Suffice to say here that it is an ancient and beautiful town, physically dominated by the ruined castle and magnificent parish church, on the A49, 27 miles S. of Shrewsbury.

Richard Baxter (1615-1691) was educated, or supposedly educated, by Richard Wickstead at Ludlow Castle.

Samuel Butler (1612-1680), author of the great satire **Hudibras** (1663-1678) was Steward at the castle in the year 1661.

A. E. Housman (1859-1936) referred nostalgically to Ludlow in many of his Shropshire poems. His ashes were buried near the north door of St. Laurence's Church.

John Milton (1608-1674) wrote the masque **Comus** (1634) in honour of the Earl of

View of Ludlow from the Whitcliffe.

Bridgewater and it was performed for the first time in the Council Chamber of Ludlow Castle.

Philip Sidney (1554-1586) often visited Ludlow Castle as a child, his father being Lord President of the Council of the Marches.

Stanley Weyman (1855-1928) was Ludlow's own novelist. He was born at 54. Broad Street and lived in the town until the 1890's.

Thomas Wright (1810-1877) the antiquarian was educated at Ludlow Grammar School.

Francis Brett Young (1884-1954) the Worcestershire novelist knew Ludlow and the surrounding area well and used the town as a setting for part of **The Iron Age** (1916).

LUTWYCHE HALL

On the B4371, 5½ miles SW. of Much Wenlock. Birthplace of the novelist Stella Benson (1892-1933).

LYTH HILL

Off the A49, 4 miles SW. of Shrewsbury. This was a favourite haunt of Mary Webb (1881-1927) and she lived here at Spring Cottage from 1917 until her death.

MADELEY

Former industrial town, now part of Telford, on the A442, 6 miles SE. of Wellington.

Joseph Anstice (1808-1836) the essayist and scholar was born at Madeley Wood Hall.

John Fletcher (1729-1785) the great preacher and friend of John Wesley was vicar here for many years up to his death.

John Randall (1810-1910) was a prolific writer and publisher who was born in Madeley and kept the Post Office in Park Avenue.

John Wesley (1703-1791) was a regular visitor of his friend John Fletcher at Madeley Vicarage. Wesley often preached in the old church and at Madeley Wood.

MARTON

Village on the B4386, 15 miles SW. of Shrewsbury. Thomas Bray (1658-1730), founder of the S.P.C.K. was born here at Marton Crest.

MEOLE BRACE

Village on the SW. outskirts of Shrewsbury. Just off the A5. The children's author Lucy Bather (1836-1864) lived at the Hall up to the time of her premature death. Gavin Gibbons (1922-1978) lived in the village latterly and Mary Webb (1888-1927) lived at Maesbrook, a large house which was demolished before the last war, from 1902 until her marriage in 1912.

MINSTERLEY

On the A488, 9 miles SW. of Shrewsbury, Minsterley has a beautiful half-timbered manor house and an unusual church both of which are connected with the Thynne family. The Thynnes originated from Caus Castle but moved to Minsterley after the

Spring Cottage, Lyth Hill.

failure of that township. William Thynne (?-1546) was the first editor of Chaucer's works. The family had the village church built in the seventeenth century in a semi-Baroque style. Inside the church are a number of maidens' garlands, rather sad and poignant remnants of a custom which died out at the end of the eighteenth century. In Shakespeare's **Hamlet**, it may be remembered, Ophelia was allowed to have such garlands or crants at her funeral in spite of the disapproval of the priest.

MUCH WENLOCK

Picturesque old town built largely of the mellow local limestone, on the A458, 13 miles SE. of Shrewsbury. Two of its most prominent features are the ruins of St. Milburga's Priory and the ancient Guildhall. Catherine Milnes Gaskell (1857-1935), a writer herself, lived at Wenlock Abbey which adjoins the Priory. Among her literary visitors over the years were Thomas Hardy (1840-1928) and his wife Emma and Henry James (1843-1916). Mary Webb (1881-1927) spent part of her childhood at The Grange, a large house on the Church Stretton road.

MYDDLE

Village on a minor road just to the W. of the A528, 8 miles NW. of Shrewsbury. There are a few remains of the thirteenth century castle on farmland behind the church. The village has been made famous by Richard Gough (1635-1723) whose **History of Myddle** has become virtually a classic of social and historical documentation.

NEWPORT

Busy market town on the A41 and A518, 18 miles ENE. of Shrewsbury. Thomas Brown (1663-1704) the irreverent satirist is thought to have been born here and was certainly educated at Newport Grammar School. Charles Dickens (1812-1870) stayed at The Bear Hotel, now called Beaumaris House and part of the Grammar School. A little further north is Chetwynd House, formerly the home of Elizabeth Parker, the recluse on whom Dickens modelled Miss Havisham in **Great Expectations** (1861).

OSWESTRY

Market town on the A483, 18 miles NW. of Shrewsbury and close to the Welsh border. Close by is the ancient earthwork known as Old Oswestry, a massive Iron Age hill fort covering nearly forty acres.

Shirley Brooks (1816-1874) the novelist and editor lived and worked in the town as a young man.

Isaac Hughes (1809-1881) was an Oswestry poet and shoemaker.

Wilfred Owen (1893-1918), arguably the finest poet of the First World War, was born at a house called Plas Wilmot in Weston Lane.

Thomas Netherton Parker (died 1848), gentlemen writer, lived at Sweeney Hall.

Barbara Pym (1913-1980), the highly acclaimed novelist, was born at 72. Willow Street and lived for many years at the family home, Morda Lodge in Morda Road.

Richard Richards (19th century), schoolmaster and minor poet, kept schools in Croxon's Square and Willow Street.

Beaumaris House, Newport, formerly the Bear Inn.

The ornate chimneys at Plaish Hall.

William Archibald Spooner (1844-1930), best known for his lapses of speech known as Spoonerisms, was educated at Oswestry School.

OTELEY

A nineteenth century mansion house close to The Mere, Ellesmere. The original house (now demolished) was the birthplace of the poet Sir Francis Kynaston (1587-1642).

PLAISH HALL

Plaish is a tiny village on a minor road, 5 miles NE. of Church Stretton. William Leighton (active 1603-1614), the composer and poet, lived at Plaish Hall. It is one of the earliest examples of a brick built house in the county, built for his father, also named William, who was a Chief Justice. Legend has it that he employed a man whom he had previously condemned to death to build the fine ornate chimneys, with the promise of freedom if the chimneys proved to be the finest in Shropshire. Not surprisingly the prisoner kept his side of the bargain, built the beautifully ornate and twisted chimneys and was hanged for his pains by order of the untrustworthy Chief Justice Leighton. The more lurid versions of the story claim that he was hanged from one of the chimneys but whether this is true or not his ghost is said to haunt Plaish Hall to this day. The infamous judge incidentally lies in Cardington Church a mile or two from Plaish – the tomb has a life size effigy of the Chief Justice lying stiffly on his side and one cannot but hope that he is as uncomfortable as he looks!

PLOWDEN HALL

Just off the A489, 4 miles ESE. of Bishop's Castle. It is an Elizabethan timber-framed house and is described by Joseph Henry Shorthouse (1834-1903) in his novel **John Inglesant** (1881).

PONTESBURY

Village on the A488, 8 miles SW. of Shrewsbury. D. H. Lawrence (1885-1930) visited a friend, Frederick Carter, at his Pontesbury home in 1924 and later depicted local scenes and people in his short novel **St. Mawr** (1925). Mary Webb (1881-1927) lived here with her husband Henry [pen name Henry Clayton (qv)] at Rose Cottage in Hinton Lane and wrote her first novel **The Golden Arrow** (1916). They later rented a cottage near to the village at The Nills.

RATLINGHOPE

Isolated village between the Stiperstones and Longmynd ranges, 4 miles NW. of Church Stretton. Called Slepe in the novels of Mary Webb (1881-1927).

ROWTON

Village off the A442, 6 miles NNW. of Wellington. Richard Baxter (1615-1691) was born here and spent his early childhood in the village before moving to Eaton Constantine.

RUYTON-OF-THE-ELEVEN-TOWNS

Village on the B4397, approximately 8 miles SE. of Oswestry. The young Arthur Conan Doyle (1859-1930) worked here for four months in 1878 as medical assistant to Dr. Elliot.

SELATTYN

Upland village, close to Offa's Dyke, with views over the Shropshire and Welsh hills, on the B4579. The village is about 3 miles NW. of Oswestry. The Welsh language poet Goronwy Owen (1723-1769?) was curate here for a time before moving to Uppington.

SHIFNAL

Small town on the A464 containing many ancient and attractive buildings, 17 miles ESE. of Shrewsbury. The bibliographer Beriah Botfield (1807-1863) lived at nearby Decker Hall and the satirist Thomas Brown (1663-1704) may have been born in the town. Charles Dickens (1812-1870) passed through on one of his visits to Shropshire

View of Shrewsbury School from The Quarry.

while Mary Augusta Ward (1851-1920), better known as Mrs. Humphrey Ward, spent three or four less than idyllic years in Shifnal as a pupil at the Rock Terrace School For Young Ladies. P. G. Wodehouse (1881-1975) knew this part of the county well and it seems likely that Shifnal was the place he had in mind for his fictional Market Blandings.

SHREWSBURY

In his novel **Howard's End** (1910) E. M. Forster (1879-1970) refers to Shrewsbury as "... the astonishing city ...". It remains astonishing to this day, in spite of the ravages of developers and so-called planners in the 1950's and 1960's, for its wealth of mediaeval and Tudor buildings, for its great sense of history and, above all, for its situation in an almost circular loop of the River Severn. Not surprisingly then many famous, and infamous, figures have arrived at this county town over the centuries and among them have been writers, many of whom are listed here.

Richard Harris Barham (1788-1845) was author of the **Ingoldsby Legends** (1840) in which he perpetuated the name of the famous Shrewsbury Cake.

William Henry West Betty (1791-1874) the famous child actor was born in the town.

Charles Burney (1726-1814), author and musician, was born in Raven Street (later called Castle Street).

The Raven Hotel, Shrewsbury. Overleaf – view of Shrewsbury from the English Bridge.

109

Samuel Butler (1835-1902) was educated at Shrewsbury School.

Neville Cardus (1889-1975), the music critic and cricket writer, was assistant cricket coach and later secretary to the headmaster at Shrewsbury School before the First World War.

Thomas Churchyard (1520-1604), poet, soldier and courtier, was born in Shrewsbury.

Desmond Coke (1879-1959) was educated at Shrewsbury School and recalled it in one of his stories for boys.

Samuel Taylor Coleridge (1772-1834) was in Shrewsbury in 1797 as a locum at the High Street Unitarian Church.

Charles Robert Darwin (1809-1882) was born at Mount House and educated at a school at 13 Claremont Hill and later Shrewsbury School. His statue stands outside the old school buildings at Castle Gates (now Shrewsbury Library).

Daniel Defoe (1660-1731) visited the town on one of his tours and described his impressions of the place.

Thomas De Quincey (1785-1859) stayed at The Lion Hotel and passed a very restless night in that establishment.

Charles Dickens (1812-1870) also stayed at The Lion Hotel and performed at the Music Hall on three occasions.

Benjamin Disraeli (1804-1881), the great statesman and novelist, was M.P. for Shrewsbury from 1841 to 1847.

John F. M. Dovaston (1782-1854) was educated at Shrewsbury School.

Frances Eagar (died 1978) lived latterly at Ingram's Hall, The Schools.

George Farquahar (1678-1707) visited Shrewsbury as an army officer and set his play **The Recruiting Officer** (1706) in the town.

Celia Fiennes (1662-1741) visited Shrewsbury in 1698.

Gavin Gibbons (1922-1978) was educated at Shrewsbury School and made his home in Shrewsbury.

Fulke Greville (1554-1628), author and nobleman, was a contemporary of Sir Philip Sidney at Shrewsbury School.

Nathaniel Hawthorne (1804-1864), the important American writer, visited in 1855 and stayed at The Lion Hotel.

William Walsham How (1823-1897), author and hymn writer, was born at College Hill and educated at Shrewsbury School.

Charles Hulbert (1778-1857) came to Shrewsbury from Manchester, ran a cotton factory and turned to literature both as a writer and as a publisher and printer.

Ernest George Lee (1896-?), author of religious works and a novel, was minister at the High Street Unitarian Church in the 1930's.

Arthur Mainwaring (1668-1712), poet and critic, was educated at Shrewsbury School.

Eliza Meteyard (1816-1879) was born in Shrewsbury.

Bruce Montgomery (1921-1978) taught at Shrewsbury School and wrote detective novels under the name Edmund Crispin.

Job Orton (1717-1783) was born in Shrewsbury, educated at Shrewsbury School and was yet another influential figure to be connected with the High Street Unitarian Church.

Wilfred Owen (1893-1918), possibly the finest of all war poets, spent the latter part of

71 Monkmoor Road, one time home of Wilfred Owen.

his childhood and his teenage years living in Shrewsbury with his parents at 1 Cleveland Place and, later, 71 Monkmoor Road.

Ambrose Philips (c.1675-1749) was a controversial poet born in Shrewsbury and educated, like so many others, at Shrewsbury School.

The novelist Lester Ralph (1878-1936) taught at the Priory School for Boys from 1914 onwards.

David Simons (19th century), was an aspiring Welsh poet who made himself unpopular, to say the least, with his scurrilous newspaper in Shrewsbury.

Mary Webb (1881-1927), Shropshire's own novelist and poet, had a stall in the market for a time during the First World War. She lived at Meole Brace on the outskirts of the town and obviously knew and loved Shrewsbury, which she called Silverton in her novels.

John Wesley (1703-1791) visited and preached in Shrewsbury on several occasions. On his first visit he preached from 1 Fish Street, a building which is now called Wesley House.

John Bickerton Williams (1792-1855) was Mayor of Shrewsbury in 1836.

Robert Williams (1810-1881), the linguist, was educated at Shrewsbury School.

Bear Steps, Shrewsbury. "And there are passages opening under archways, and winding up between high edifices, very tempting to the explorer, and generally leading to some court, or some queer old range of buildings . . . " Nathaniel Hawthorne (1804-1864).

STABLEFORD

Village on a minor road off the B4176, approximately 5 miles NE. of Bridgnorth. The novelist P. G. Wodehouse spent holidays here at Hay's House during his teenage years and came to know neighbouring villages in this attractive eastern part of the county.

STANTON-ON-HINE-HEATH

Village on a minor road off the A53, 9 miles NE. of Shrewsbury. Mary Webb (1881-1927) lived here with her parents from 1896 to 1902 before moving to Meole Brace. Their home was a large house just beyond the village called The Woodlands (now a private house re-named Harcourt Manor).

STIPERSTONES

A bleak upland plateau extending for several miles S. of Pontesbury, roughly parallel with the A488. The whole area has been mined for lead and other minerals since Roman times and today there are still gaunt, derelict remains of engine houses and chimney stacks to be seen around the fringes of the plateau. The Stiperstones are capped by great outcrops of rock, the most famous of which is known as the Devil's

The Devil's Chair, Stiperstones; the setting for part of D. H. Lawrence's novel Saint Mawr (1925).

115

Chair. D. H. Lawrence (1885-1930) used the Stiperstones and the Devil's Chair in particular as a setting for part of his novel **St. Mawr** (1925). Mary Webb (1888-1927) knew the area intimately, called the Stiperstones the Diafol Mountains in her fiction and, in **The Golden Arrow** (1916), gave us memorable descriptions of this strange and inhospitable place.

STOKESAY CASTLE

Generally considered the finest mediaeval fortified manor house in the country and one of Shropshire's jewels, Stokesay Castle lies just off the A49, 6½ miles NW. of Ludlow. The American novelist Henry James (1843-1916) came here and described his sense of enchantment with what he saw in **English Hours** (1875).

TERN HALL

A former early eighteenth century house which was incorporated into Attingham Hall when it was built in the 1780's. Attingham lies in its own extensive parkland off the A5, 4½ miles SE. of Shrewsbury. The great preacher John Fletcher (1729-1785) was a private tutor at Tern Hall before he moved to Madeley.

Stokesay Castle Gatehouse, described by Henry James in his book English Hours (1875).

Tong Church was described by Charles Dickens in The Old Curiosity Shop (1841).

116

TONG

Picturesque village on the A41, 3 miles E. of Shifnal. Charles Dickens (1812-1870) stayed here and described the village and the church in **The Old Curiosity Shop** (1841). The antiquarian Robert William Eyton (1815-1881) spent much of his childhood at Tong.

TRENCH FARM

On a minor road off the A5113, 1½ miles S. of Wem. John Ireland (died 1808), the biographer of Hogarth, was born and brought up here. William Wycherley (1640-1746), the great Restoration dramatist, spent much of his childhood here since it was part of his father's extensive property.

UFFINGTON

Village on a minor road off the B5062, 2 miles ENE. of Shrewsbury. Wilfred Owen (1893-1918) and his family often worshipped at the church here on Sundays in the summer having walked from their home in Monkmoor Road, Shrewsbury and crossed the river to Uffington by the ferry.

UPPINGTON

Delightful village with beautiful avenues of trees on its approaches lying off the A5, 4 miles W. of Wellington. The theologian Richard Allestree (1619-1681) was born here and the Welsh language poet Goronwy Owen (1723-1769?) was curate at the church from 1748 to 1753.

UPTON MAGNA

Village on a minor road some way off the A5, 4 miles E. of Shrewsbury. The children's writer and biographer E. M. Almedingen (1898-1971) lived just outside the village, on the road to Atcham, at a house called Frogmore.

WELLINGTON

Busy town, traditionally the capital of the east Shropshire industrial district, on the A5, 11 miles E. of Shrewsbury.
Patrick Bronte (1777-1861) was curate at All Saints' Church in 1809 before moving to Yorkshire.
Philip Larkin (1922-1985) the highly acclaimed poet began his career in librarianship at Wellington from 1943 to 1946.
William Vincent Moorhouse (early 19th century) lived here and his poems were published by Houlstons of Market Square.
Mary Martha Sherwood (1775-1851) had a long association with Houlstons who published many of her moral tales for children.
Hesba Stretton (1832-1911), best selling author of children's stories, was born in New Street and educated at the Old Hall School.

WEM

Small town on the A5113, 10 miles E. of Shrewsbury. William Hazlitt (1778-1830), the essayist and critic, spent much of his early life in Wem and lived with his parents in Noble Street. John Bickerton Williams (1792-1855) retired to The Hall, a Georgian house in New Street.

WENLOCK EDGE

Beautiful wooded escarpment running SW. for 4 miles or so from Much Wenlock. Immortalised by A. E. Housman (1859-1936) in one of his most famous poems from **A Shropshire Lad** (1896).

WEST FELTON

Village on the A5, 15 miles NW. of Shrewsbury. John F. M. Dovaston (1782-1854) was born here at a house called The Nursery and lived here for most of his life. John Bickerton Williams (1792-1855) was also born in this village which is passed by most motorists without a second thought. Turn off the main road and into the village proper and its charms will be seen in full.

WESTON PARK

Lying off the A5, 10 miles E. of Wellington, the Hall itself and much of the park is actually in Staffordshire. However, part does spread into Shropshire and is included here as it is a possible location for the fictional Blandings Castle in the novels of P. G. Wodehouse (1881-1975).

WHITCHURCH

Once described in the Town Guide as "Gateway to the North" (shades of Peter Sellers' "Balham, gateway to the South"?), Whitchurch has a long and illustrious history and does indeed stand on the main road to the north, the A41, and is 19 miles N. of Shrewsbury.

Roger Cotton (fl. 1596) was born in Alkington and educated in Whitchurch.

Daniel Defoe (1660-1731) and Celia Fiennes (1662-1741) both visited the town and recorded their impressions.

Reginald Heber (1783-1826), the hymn writer and poet, was educated at Whitchurch Grammar School.

John Talbot, Earl of Shrewsbury, was a Whitchurch man, a great soldier, whose body was brought back from Bordeaux to St. Alkmund's Church for burial after his death in battle. It was this man whose fame Shakespeare perpetuated in **King Henry VI, Part 1.**

It should also be mentioned, although he was not a literary figure as such, that the influential nineteenth century illustrator of children's books, Randolph Caldecott, was a bank clerk in Whitchurch in his youth.

WHITTINGTON

Village on the A5, 18 miles NW. of Shrewsbury with a picturesque mediaeval castle

View from Wenlock Edge.

complete with moat alongside the main road. The castle was built by the Fitzwarine family in the thirteenth century and figures in the romance called **Foulques Fitwarin.** John F. M. Dovaston (1782-1854) produced his own version of this, based on Whittington Castle, in 1812. The great hymn writer William Walsham How (1823-1897) was rector here for many years.

WILDERHOPE MANOR
Sixteenth century stone-built manor house, off the B4371 and about 7 miles SW. of Much Wenlock. Possibly the original of Undern Hall in **Gone to Earth** (1917) by Mary Webb (1888-1927), home of the moustache-twirling villain Jack Reddin.

WORFIELD
Village off the A442, 3 miles NE. of Bridgnorth. E. M. Almedingen (1898-1971) lived here in the 1920's after coming to this country from Russia.

WREKIN
Possibly Shropshire's most famous landmark, the Wrekin rises to over 1,300 feet but seems even higher from certain angles as it towers over the low lying land beneath it. Of course it has its expected quota of folk tales connected with it and has received frequent mentions in literary works of one sort or another. Perhaps it will suffice here to recall that old Shropshire toast "To all friends round the Wrekin" and note that the dramatist George Farquhar (1678-1707) used this as the dedication to his play **The Recruiting Officer** (1706).

WROXETER
Village on the B4380, 8 miles E. of Shrewsbury. Nearby are the remarkable remains of the Roman city of Uriconium. Richard Baxter (1615-1691) attended the free school at Wroxeter for a time from his home in Eaton Constantine. Charles Dickens (1812-1870) visited the Roman excavations and wrote a lengthy article in **All the Year Round.**

Whittington Castle ▶

APPENDIX 1

Supplementary list of authors and titles

AYSCOUGH, John **GRACECHURCH.** A novel set in Ellesmere.

CARR, E. Donald **A Night in the Snow** (1865)

DOD, Robert Phipps (died 1865)
Author of **Birth and Worth, an Enquiry into the Practical Use of a Pedigree** (1849), lived at Nant Issa Hall near Oswestry.

FARDO, George (nineteenth century)
Oswestry-born art critic and minor poet.

FRAUNCE, Abraham (died early seventeenth century)
Poet; born in Shropshire and thought to have been educated at Shrewsbury School.

GANDY, Ida **An Idler on the Shropshire Borders** (1970)

HUNT, Agnes (1867-1948)
Pioneering nurse and founder of the orthopaedic hospital at Gobowen. Her biography **My Life** was published in 1938.

KENYON, Katherine Mary Rose **A House That Was Loved** (1941)

'NIMROD' **Memoirs of the Life of the Late John Mytton, Esq.** (1835)

OMAN, Carola **Ayot Rectory** (1965)

PERCY, Cyril Heber **Us Four** (1963)

SALWEY, T. (nineteenth century)
Vicar of Oswestry in the 1840's and 1850's and minor poet. **Gospel Hymns** was published in 1847.

TAYLOR, John (1580-1653)
Poet; born in Gloucester. Taylor celebrated Thomas Parr ('Old Parr') of Alberbury in Shropshire in one of his poems. Parr was reputed to have lived from 1483 to 1635, a somewhat doubtful claim but one which brought him a great deal of fame.

WILDE, OSCAR (1854-1900)
His popular play **The Importance of Being Earnest** (1899) contains many references to Shropshire where the character John Worthing tells us he has neighbours who are "Perfectly horrid!" and where his friend Algernon Moncrieff claims to have "Bunburyed . . . on two separate occasions".

APPENDIX 2

Buildings open to the public at sites mentioned in the text. Readers are advised to check opening times, etc., with the local tourist information office before visiting.

ATTINGHAM PARK
Atcham

Open March to October, admission charge, access for wheelchairs.

BRIDGNORTH
BISHOP PERCY'S HOUSE

Viewing by appointment only, donations appreciated.

CLUN CASTLE

Open at all times, no charge.

CONDOVER HALL
Royal National Institute for the Blind

Limited viewing during August only, no charge.

HAUGHMOND ABBEY

Open all year round, charge for admission, access for wheelchairs.

LILLESHALL ABBEY

Open Easter to September, admission charge, access for wheelchairs.

LUDLOW CASTLE

Open April to October, winter opening on application, admission charge.

SHREWSBURY LIBRARY,
CASTLE GATES
(Original Shrewsbury School)

Open normal library hours, no charge.

STOKESAY CASTLE

Open all year round with limited opening hours in November, closed Thursdays, admission charge.

WESTON PARK
Near Shifnal

Open March to September at varying times, admission charge, advisable to check opening hours before going.

WHITTINGTON CASTLE

Open at all times.

WILDERHOPE MANOR

Open March to September on certain days, limited during winter months, admission charge.

WROXETER
(Uriconium)

Open all year round, admission charge and access for wheelchairs.

MAP OF SHROPSHIRE

(by J. Dickins)

125

SELECT BIBLIOGRAPHY

BOASE, P. **Modern English Biography** (1965)
CARDUS, Neville **Autobiography** (1947)
CARPENTER, Maurice **Samuel Taylor Coleridge: the indifferent horseman** (1954)
CHAMBERS BIOGRAPHICAL DICTIONARY (1984)
COLES, Gladys Mary **The Flower of Light** (1978)
CONNELY, Willard **Brawny Wycherley** (1930)
CUTT, M. Nancy **Mrs. Sherwood and her books for children** (1974)
THE DICTIONARY OF NATIONAL BIOGRAPHY (1882)
EAGLE, Dorothy and CARNELL, Hilary **The Oxford Literary Guide to the British Isles** (1977)
GILL, Frederick C. **In the steps of John Wesley** (1962)
GRAVES, Richard Perceval **A. E. Housman: the scholar poet** (1979)
HARDWICK, Michael **A literary atlas and gazetteer of the British Isles** (1973)
HARVEY, Paul (ed.) **The Oxford Companion to English Literature** (1967)
KUNITZ, Stanley J. and HAYCRAFT, Howard **British authors before 1800** (1952), **British authors of the 19th century** (1936), **Twentieth century authors** (1942)
LLOYD, David and KLEIN, Peter **Ludlow: a historic town in words and pictures** (1984)
MACLEAN, Catherine Macdonald **Born under Saturn: a biography of William Hazlitt** (1965)
MEE, Arthur **Shropshire** (1968)
MOORE, Harry Tyler **The intelligent heart** (1955)
MOULDER, Michael **Shropshire: a Shell guide** (1973)
MURPHY, N. T. P. **In search of Blandings** (1981)
NUTTALL, Geoffrey F. **Richard Baxter** (1965)
OXFORD COMPANION TO CHILDREN'S LITERATURE (1984)
PEELE, Michael **Shropshire in poem and legend** (1923)
PEVSNER, Nikolaus **Shropshire** (1958)
PYM, Barbara **A very private eye** (1984)
SACKVILLE WEST, Edward **A flame in sunlight: the life and work of Thomas de Quincey** (1936)
THE SHROPSHIRE MAGAZINE
STALLWORTHY, Jon **Wilfred Owen** (1974)
STILLMAN, Clara C. **Samuel Butler** (1932)
WARD, A. C. **The Longman companion to twentieth century literature** (1970)
WHO WAS WHO (1967)
WRENN, Dorothy P. H. **Goodbye to morning** (1964), **Shropshire history makers** (1975)

ILLUSTRATIONS

ILLUSTRATIONS (Cont.)